# fitness
## on a plate

### anita bean's
GUIDE TO HEALTHY EATING

First published 2003 by
A & C Black Publishers Ltd
37 Soho Square, London W1D 3QZ
www.acblack.com

Copyright © 2003 Anita Bean

ISBN 0 7136 6381 2

A CIP catalogue record for this book is available
from the British Library.

Note: Whilst every effort has been made to ensure
that the content of this book is technically
accurate and as sound as possible, neither the
author nor the publishers can accept responsibility
for any injury or loss sustained as a result of use
of this material.

Text and cover design by Jocelyn Lucas
Cover and inside photographs © Comstock, Inc.
Back cover photograph © Imagestate
Illustration on p. 2 © Tina Howe
Author photograph by Grant Pritchard

A & C Black uses paper produced with elemental
chlorine-free pulp, harvested from managed
sustainable forests.

Printed and bound in Singapore by
Tien Wah Press (Pte.) Ltd

# contents

# acknowledgements

I thank my husband Simon for his eternal optimism and never-ending support, and my two beautiful daughters, Chloe and Lucy for their love of life, all of which gives me the inspiration to write this book.

I would like to thank everyone who has shared their valuable experience and knowledge with me during the writing of this book; exercise physiologist and Director of Human Performance at Lilleshall National Sports Centre, John Brewer; conditioning expert, Clive Brewer (no relation); personal trainer and friend, Lee Mason; former Fulham football player Tom Upsher; fitness instructor, David Eatock; exercise specialist Kesh Patel; marathon runner, Susie Whalley; Commonwealth gymnastics champion, Kaj Jackson; nutritionist Rachel Ann Hill; and my fit friends Andy Jackson, Sarah Plant, and Paul and Alison Nicholls.

A big thank you to top photographer Grant Pritchard, Holmes Place Epsom for the location, and make-up artist Toni at Re-Aqua.

Last but not least, many thanks to my editors Charlotte Jenkins and Hannah McEwen and the rest of the team at A & C Black.

# introduction

Congratulations! By picking up this book you have taken an important step towards achieving a leaner, healthier body. You are about to discover how to eat for maximising your fitness and increasing your energy. If you're serious about getting into shape, you need the right kind of fuel that meets the tough demands of your fitness programme.

I have been advising regular exercisers for 15 years and I know that what, how much and when you eat have a big effect on performance and recovery. Get the balance right and you'll have plenty of energy to train. But without the right fuel you simply won't keep up the pace.

It always amazes me how many exercisers leave their diet to chance. Knowing what to eat and drink before, during and after working out will allow you get the most out of your fitness programme. Whether you train in the gym, run, cycle or swim, you'll benefit from making some easy changes to your eating habits.

One of the most common questions I get asked is how to lose fat and build muscle. These goals can only be achieved by careful eating combined with consistent training. Fail to plan your diet properly and you'll never get lean no matter how hard you train. Here, you'll learn how to adapt your eating and training to get the physique you want.

I am also constantly asked whether there are special foods or supplements that can enhance your performance or make you burn more fat. Here, I'll give you the low-down on all those the sports foods, drinks and supplements and tell you which ones work - and which ones are a waste of time.

While the main nutritional messages apply to most fitness activities, one size doesn't always fit all. In this book, I have prepared specific advice for gym goers, runners, cyclists and swimmers. I'll tell you how to tailor your diet to the exact requirements of your activity whether you are training for fitness or competition. I'm also happy to pass on lots of great tips from fellow athletes, coaches and fitness experts who have been kind enough to impart their experience.

Here's to a great workout!

## Anita

# what should you be eating?

It's a fact that people who work-out regularly have different nutritional needs from the average couch potato. Everyone needs to eat a balanced diet to keep healthy and avoid illness, but as a regular exerciser you need a diet that meets the tough demands of your training programme as well as one that keeps your body in peak condition. Get the right balance and you'll have more energy and vitality to train and live life to the full.

## the fitness food pyramid

The healthy eating guidelines designed for the general population – including the Health Department Agency's *National Food Guide* and the US Department of Agriculture's *Food Guide Pyramid* – are not wholly appropriate for regular exercisers. You need an eating plan more finely tuned to your workout lifestyle.

That's why I have designed the Fitness Food Pyramid to give you a better base upon which to plan your diet. It expands the number of food groups from five to six, incorporating healthy fats and further emphasises fruit and vegetables by placing them at the base of the pyramid. Eating this way means that you will be getting more vitamins, minerals, antioxidants and phytonutrients (see page 15) than non-active people – nutrients that are vital for keeping your body in peak health. The Fitness Food Pyramid also gives you realistic portion guidance to help you construct a healthier diet that is better suited to your active lifestyle.

## how the fitness food pyramid works

Each food group provides some, but not all, of the nutrients you need for keeping fit and healthy. You should eat a variety of foods within each

**junk food**
up to 1 portion a day
or in moderation

**healthy fats**
1–2 portions a day

**protein-rich foods**
2–4 portions a day

**calcium-rich foods**
2–4 portions a day

**carbohydrate-rich foods**
4–6 portions a day

**vegetables**
3–5
portions
a day

**fruit**
2–4
portions
a day

group and aim to eat roughly the recommended number of portions each day.

As you can see, the foods in the lower layers of the pyramid – fruit, vegetables and carbohydrate-rich foods – should form the main part of your diet, while those at the top – healthy fats and junk foods – should be eaten in smaller quantities.

That's not to say that you should concentrate only on the lower layers or dismiss the smaller layers. Each food group is equally important. You need to get the balance right.

The more varied your diet overall, the more likely you are to get all the nutrients you need. It may seem easier to stick to the same meals day after day but you could end up missing out on some nutrients. Eating lots of one or two kinds of food – even if it's fresh fruit or raw salad – doesn't make a balanced diet. You may be missing out on other vital nutrients such as protein or calcium.

## case study

Steve Keen is a competitive runner and regular gym goer. He trains four times a week, either in the gym or running outdoors, and leads a relatively healthy and stress-free lifestyle. He asked me for advice on his diet as he was getting frequent colds and feeling run-down, despite eating what he thought was a healthy diet.

As it turned out, Steve was eating plenty of pasta, rice, fish and chicken – the mainstays of the typical athlete's diet – but he was eating very few fresh vegetables. The processed tomato in the pasta sauce was usually his only vegetable of the day! He also relied heavily on 'white' or refined carbohydrate foods (such as white pasta) instead of whole grains, which meant he was missing out on important antioxidant minerals. It was apparent that Steve wasn't getting enough beta-carotene, vitamin C and phytonutrients, which almost certainly resulted in his low resistance to viruses and frequent colds.

I advised him to include a fresh vegetable or salad with each main meal, to snack on fruit twice daily and swap his white pasta and rice for wholegrain varieties. He also began taking multivitamin and antioxidant supplements to boost his immunity. I am pleased to report that after three months, Steve has remained free from colds, and is now able to train harder than he had before.

# what's a portion?

| food group | portion size |
| --- | --- |
| fruit | **1 piece about the size of a tennis ball** |
| | • 1 medium fruit, e.g. apple, orange, banana, peach |
| | • 2 small fruits, e.g. kiwi fruit, plums, satsumas, apricots |

- 1 cupful of berries, e.g. strawberries, raspberries, cherries, grapes
- 1 large slice of large fruit, e.g. melon, mango, pineapple

**vegetables**

**about the amount you can hold in your hand, 80g, or:**

- 1 dessert bowl of salad vegetables, e.g. lettuce, salad leaves
- 2 tablespoons of cooked vegetables, e.g. broccoli, cauliflower, carrots, green beans, peppers, peas, mange tout

**carbohydrate-rich foods**

- 1 portion pasta, rice, grains, cereal, pulses, the size of your palm
- 1 baked potato, the size of your clenched fist
- 2 slices bread
- 1 roll or bagel or tortilla

**calcium-rich foods**

- milk, 1 cup
- yoghurt, 1 carton
- cheese, 4 dice

**protein-rich foods**

- Meat, poultry, fish, quorn, tofu, size of deck of cards
- pulses, size of your palm
- 2 eggs

**healthy fats**

- Olive, rapeseed, walnut, flax seed oil = 2 teaspoons
- ½ avocado
- nuts and seeds, 2 tablespoons
- oily fish, deck of cards size

## vegetables and fruit

*3–5 portions of vegetables a day*
*2–4 portions of fruit a day*

Fruit and vegetables provide vitamins, minerals, fibre and phyto-nutrients (see page 15), which are vital for peak health. A high level of fruit and vegetables in your diet helps to boost your immunity and protect your body from cancer, heart disease and bowel disease. Try to buy fruit and vegetables that have been grown locally (not imported), that are in season and are not damaged or discoloured in any way. You may need to shop more than once a week, as many fresh foods don't keep for more than a few days. Food starts to lose its vitamins once it is exposed to air and light so store vegetables and soft fruits in a cool, dark place. Cut and prepare fruit and vegetables just before using them. When you cook vegetables, try steaming them over a little boiling water so that they retain most of their vitamins. If you must boil your vegetables, use only a little water (about 1–2 cm) and add them to the pan only once the water has come to the boil. Cook them until they are only just tender, not soft and soggy. Stir-frying is also a good cooking method as the food is cooked in a little oil at a high temperature for a brief time, so the vitamins are kept sealed in.

### orange, pineapple and banana smoothie

*Smoothies are a great way of adding extra fruit and valuable fluid to your diet. Not only do they pack a nutritional punch, they are free from artificial sweeteners and preservatives. They are ideal pre-workout drinks (about an hour before your workout) as well as drinking post-workout. Try this delicious combination of fresh fruit.*

**makes 2 drinks**
200 ml (7 fl oz) orange juice
200 g (7 oz) fresh pineapple, cut into pieces
2 bananas cut into chunks
A few ice cubes

- Place the ice cubes in the goblet of a smoothie maker, blender or food processor and process until slushy.
- Add the orange juice, pineapple and banana and then process for about 45 seconds until smooth. Serve immediately.

## *here are some tips when buying fresh food:*

- buy seasonal varieties of fruit and vegetables when they are cheaper and fresher
- if you want to try organic food, start with salads, fruit and vegetables – of all the food groups these have the highest pesticide residues so buying organic is the best way to avoid them
- wash non-organic fruit and vegetables thoroughly (ideally in a mild detergent solution, then rinse). Peeling will remove the surface residues but, unfortunately, also takes away a lot of the vitamins that are concentrated beneath the surface

### ORGANIC OR NOT?

*It is more important that you choose good quality fresh produce; whether organic or not.*

Whether organic foods are better for your health and whether they are worth paying more for is debatable. Here are the facts to help you make up your mind:

**1** Several studies have found that organic food contains vitamin C, magnesium and iron than non-organic food, but the difference isn't huge.

**2** There is no evidence to date that people who eat organic food live longer or enjoy better health than those who don't. However, a Scottish study found higher levels of salicylic acid (a natural substance that protects against cancer, stroke and heart attacks) in soup made from organic vegetables when compared with soup made from non-organic vegetables.

**3** Organic foods contain fewer contaminants such as pesticides, antibiotics and nitrates, which suggests that they are safer to eat. However, the Government's Pesticide Residues Committee say that the majority of non-organic food is safe too as any pesticide residues fall below the safety limit. Their 2002 report found that only 1 in 100 potato samples and 1 in 20 nectarines breached safety limits. However, pesticide traces were still detected in 11 out of 15 of the most popular fruit and vegetables.

## carbohydrate-rich foods

*4–6 portions a day*

This group includes foods rich in complex carbohydrates; bread, breakfast cereal, rice, pasta, porridge oats, beans, lentils and potatoes. Carbohydrate is the most important fuel for exercise as well as daily living. If you workout regularly, you need to keep your glycogen (stored carbohydrate) levels high in order to train hard. Low glycogen levels result in flagging energy, fatigue and under-par performance.

The foods in this group are also major sources of fibre, B vitamins (such as thiamin and niacin) and minerals (such as iron). Focus on the wholegrain or unrefined varieties – wholemeal bread, breakfast cereals, pasta and rice – rather than refined 'white' versions, which have been largely stripped of vitamins, minerals and fibre.

Try to include several different carbohydrate foods in your daily diet. That may sound obvious, but it's surprising how many people rely on wheat to the exclusion of other grains. Wholewheat products are nutritious but you'll get further benefits by including other grain varieties (such as oats, brown rice, millet and quinoa) and starchy vegetables, such as ordinary and sweet potatoes.

## calcium-rich foods

*2–4 portions a day*

Including dairy products – milk, cheese, yoghurt and fromage frais – in your daily diet is the easiest way to get calcium, which is needed for strong bones and teeth. As a bonus, you'll also be getting protein and B vitamins. If you don't like dairy foods, make sure you choose alternative calcium sources, such as almonds, dark green vegetables, tinned fish with soft bones, calcium-fortified products, pulses and figs.

## protein-rich foods

*2–4 portions a day*

Regular exercisers need more protein than inactive people. This is especially important if you train with weights or include other strength or power activities in your training programme. Without enough protein, you'll take longer to recover after training and your strength and muscle gains will be slower. Include modest amounts of protein-rich foods –

lean meat, poultry, fish, eggs, soya and quorn – in your daily diet. These foods are also good sources of B vitamins, iron and zinc. Vegetarians may also count beans, lentils and dairy foods toward their protein target. Protein supplements can also be included in this group if you struggle to get enough protein from your food (see pages 83 and 88).

## healthy fats
*1–2 portions a day*

The oils found in nuts, seeds, rapeseed oil, olive oil, flax seed linseed oil, sunflower oil and oily fish are especially good for regular exercisers. They contain essential fats, called omega-3 and omega-6 fatty acids, which can improve endurance as well as protect against heart disease (see 'Be fat friendly' on page 14). Pumpkin seeds and flax seeds are particularly rich in the omega-3 oils, which are lacking in most people's diets. Flax seeds have a very tough outer husk, which is practically impenetrable by digestive enzymes, so you'll need to grind them in a coffee grinder to benefit from the oils. Add to muesli, yoghurt, shakes and smoothies. Use omega-3 rich cold-pressed oils in dressings or stir a spoonful into soups and sauces. Don't fry with these oils, as high temperatures will reduce their nutritional value. To achieve the optimal intake of essential fats, you can eat:

- a portion of oily fish, such as mackerel or salmon, twice a week;
  or
- around a heaped tablespoon of nuts or seeds a day;
  or
- about 1 level tablespoon of rapeseed oil, extra virgin olive oil, flax seed oil, walnut oil, sesame oil or a mixed oil.
- a marine fish oil supplement (liquid or capsules).

## junk foods
*1 portion or less a day*

Biscuits, chocolate bars, cakes, puddings, soft drinks, sweets and crisp-like snacks supply very few essential nutrients yet lots of calories ('empty calories'). Many are loaded with artery-clogging saturated fat and hydrogenated fat (see page 16) so avoid them as far as possible. But hey, don't get too rigid here – the occasional junk food fix won't do you any harm – and may help keep your diet on track the rest of the time. A little sugar, honey or jam is also fine – use them for enhancing the flavour of healthy foods (e.g. jam on toast or porridge with honey) or for making acidic foods palatable (e.g. stewed apples or fruit crumble).

# eight things you need to know about nutrients

*Before you can get down to designing your specific eating plan, you need to know a bit more about your nutritional needs.*

## 1. not all carbohydrates are equal

All carbohydrates are turned into glucose eventually but they do this at different rates. Some carbohydrate foods produce a rapid upswing in blood glucose levels, while others give a gradual rise. In other words, not all carbs are equal. The effect various foods have on blood glucose levels is measured by the glycaemic index (GI). This is a ranking of food from 0–100 that tells you how that food will affect your blood glucose levels. Glucose has the top score of 100, which means that it produces the biggest rise in blood glucose.

Foods that break down quickly during digestion have the highest GIs. They include refined starchy foods – potatoes, corn flakes, white bread and white rice – as well as sugary foods such as soft drinks, biscuits and sweets. These foods produce a rapid rise in blood glucose. Foods that break down more slowly, releasing glucose gradually into the bloodstream, have a low GI. They include the less refined starchy foods – beans, lentils, porridge, coarse grain breads, and muesli – as well as fruit and dairy products. The GI of various foods is given in Table 1.1 on page 10.

## 2. go easy on fast carbs

Generally speaking, high GI foods produce the fastest surge of glucose in your bloodstream. Under most conditions, this energy buzz is only short-lived. What happens is that your pancreas releases insulin to transport the sugar out of the blood and into your cells. The aim is to bring your blood glucose levels back to normal. Most of the time this system works perfectly well, but if you eat lots of high glycaemic foods and this becomes your staple diet, then your system can easily become overburdened. Eventually, your cells may become desensitised to insulin, but your pancreas continues to pump out more and more in an attempt to stabilise your blood glucose. You may get energy 'highs' and 'lows' as insulin literally overcompensates for rapid blood glucose rises. This will certainly affect your training and recovery.

## 1.1 the glycaemic index and carbohydrate content of foods

| food | portion size | carbohydrate(g) | gi |
|---|---|---|---|
| *breakfast cereals* | | | |
| muesli | small bowl (50 g) | 34 | 56 |
| weetabix | 2 (40 g) | 30 | 69 |
| shredded wheat | 2 (45 g) | 31 | 67 |
| rice crispies | small bowl (30 g) | 27 | 82 |
| cornflakes | small bowl (30 g) | 26 | 84 |
| cheerios | small bowl (30 g) | 23 | 74 |
| porridge (made with water) | small bowl (160 g) | 14 | 42 |
| *grains/pasta* | | | |
| rice — brown | 6 tbsp (180 g) | 58 | 76 |
| rice — white | 6 tbsp (180 g) | 56 | 87 |
| spaghetti | 4 tbsp (220 g cooked) | 49 | 41 |
| rice — basmati | 4 tbsp (60 g) | 48 | 58 |
| pasta — macaroni | 4 tbsp (230 g cooked) | 43 | 45 |
| noodles — instant | 4 tbsp (230 g cooked) | 30 | 46 |
| *bread* | | | |
| pizza | 1 large slice (115 g) | 38 | 60 |
| white bread | 1 large slice (36 g) | 18 | 70 |
| wholemeal bread | 1 large slice (38 g) | 16 | 69 |
| *crackers/crispbreads* | | | |
| rice cakes | 1 (8 g) | 6 | 85 |
| *biscuits and cakes* | | | |
| sponge cake | 1 slice (60 g) | 39 | 46 |
| muffin | 1 (68 g) | 34 | 44 |

| | | | |
|---|---|---|---|
| digestive | 1 (15 g) | 10 | 59 |
| shortbread | 1 (13 g) | 8 | 64 |
| oatmeal | 1 (13 g) | 8 | 55 |
| rich tea | 1 (10 g) | 8 | 55 |
| *vegetables* | | | |
| chips | average portion (165 g) | 59 | 75 |
| potato – boiled, old | 2 medium (175 g) | 30 | 56 |
| potato — mashed | 4 tbsp (180 g) | 28 | 70 |
| sweet potato | 1 medium (130 g) | 27 | 54 |
| potato — boiled, new | 7 small (175 g) | 27 | 62 |
| potato — jacket | 1 average (180 g) | 22 | 85 |
| sweetcorn | 2 tbsp (85 g) | 17 | 55 |
| parsnip | 2 tbsp (65 g) | 8 | 97 |
| peas | 2 tbsp (70 g) | 7 | 48 |
| carrots | 2 tbsp (60 g) | 3 | 49 |
| *pulses* | | | |
| baked beans | 1 small tin (205 g) | 31 | 48 |
| lentils (red) | 4 tbsp (160 g) | 28 | 26 |
| chickpeas | 4 tbsp (140 g) | 24 | 33 |
| red kidney beans | 4 tbsp (120 g) | 20 | 27 |
| *fruit* | | | |
| banana | 1 (100 g) | 23 | 55 |
| raisins | 1 tbsp (30 g) | 21 | 64 |
| pear | 1 (160 g) | 16 | 38 |
| apricot (dried) | 5 (40 g) | 15 | 31 |
| grapes | small bunch (100 g) | 15 | 46 |
| apple | 1 (100 g) | 12 | 38 |
| orange | 1 (208 g) | 12 | 44 |
| mango | 1/2 (75 g) | 11 | 55 |
| cherries | small handful (100 g) | 10 | 22 |
| pineapple | 1 slice (80 g) | 8 | 66 |
| peach | 1 (121 g) | 8 | 42 |
| kiwi fruit | 1 (68 g) | 6 | 52 |
| plum | 1 (55 g) | 5 | 39 |
| apricot | 1 (40 g) | 3 | 57 |

*drinks*

| | | | |
|---|---|---|---|
| fanta | 375 ml can | 51 | 68 |
| lucozade | 250 ml bottle | 40 | 95 |
| isostar | 250 ml can | 18 | 70 |
| squash (diluted) | 250 ml glass (from 50 ml concentrate) | 14 | 66 |

*snacks*

| | | | |
|---|---|---|---|
| tortillas/corn chips | 1 bag (50 g) | 30 | 72 |
| crisps | 1 packet (30 g) | 16 | 54 |
| peanuts | small handful (50 g) | 4 | 14 |

*dairy products*

| | | | |
|---|---|---|---|
| yoghurt, fruit (low-fat) | 1 pot (150 g) | 27 | 33 |
| milk — skimmed | 1/2 pint (300 ml) | 15 | 32 |
| milk — whole | 1/2 pint (300 ml) | 14 | 27 |
| ice cream | 1 scoop (60 g) | 14 | 61 |

*confectionery*

| | | | |
|---|---|---|---|
| mars bar | 1 standard (65 g) | 43 | 68 |
| milk chocolate | 1 bar (54 g) | 31 | 49 |
| muesli bar | 1 (33 g) | 20 | 61 |

*drinks*

| | | | |
|---|---|---|---|
| apple juice | 1 glass (160 ml) | 16 | 40 |
| orange juice | 1 glass (160 ml) | 14 | 46 |

*sugars*

| | | | |
|---|---|---|---|
| honey | 1 heaped tsp (17 g) | 13 | 58 |
| glucose | 1 tsp (5 g) | 5 | 100 |
| sucrose | 1 tsp (5 g) | 5 | 65 |

**Source:** adapted from Glycaemic Index On-Line, www.glycaemicindex.com, a web site developed by the University of Sydney, Australia.

| Glycaemic Index | Colour code |
|---|---|
| 0–39 | low |
| 40–59 | moderate |
| 60–100 | high |

# 3. go for the (slow) burn

There's no need to cut out high glycaemic foods. The key is to eat them with protein and/or a little healthy fat to lower the overall glycaemic effect. Eating this way results in steadier energy levels, less fat storage and better appetite control. For example, have a bowl of cereal (high GI) with semi skimmed milk (low GI) or a slice of bread (high GI) with peanut butter (low GI). This slows the release of glucose so you get a slower burn, which is precisely what you're aiming for.

**EAT LIKE AN ATHLETE**

Studies at the University of Sydney, Australia have found that athletes produce much less insulin after eating high GI foods than would be predicted from GI tables. In other words, they don't show the same peaks and troughs in blood glucose and insulin as sedentary people do. But this doesn't give you a licence to pig out on high GI foods. Regard the GI index as a rough guide to how various foods are likely to behave in your body.

**HOW MUCH FIBRE SHOULD I HAVE?**

The Department of Health recommends between 18 g and 24 g of fibre a day, although for people prone to constipation up to 32 g a day may be a good idea. The average intake in the UK is a mere 13 g a day though. Fibre helps your digestive system work properly and is a useful ally for weight control. There are two kinds of fibre – insoluble and soluble. Most plant foods contain both, but proportions vary. Good sources of insoluble fibre include wholewheat bread and other wheat products, brown rice and vegetables. These foods help speed the passage of food through your gut, and prevent constipation and bowel problems. Soluble fibre – found in pulses, fruit and vegetables – reduces harmful LDL cholesterol levels and helps control blood glucose levels by slowing glucose absorption.

**PROTEIN FACT FILE**

Amino acids, the small components of protein, are often called the building blocks because they are used to repair muscle tissue. They are also needed for making enzymes, hormones and antibodies.

Eight of these must be provided by the diet (the 'essential amino acids'), while the body can make the others. But for your body to use food proteins properly, all eight essential amino acids have to be present. Animal proteins, as well as soya and quorn, contain a good balance of the nine essential amino acids. Plant proteins (pulses, cereals, nuts) contain smaller amounts, so these need to be combined together (e.g. beans on toast; lentils and rice; peanut butter on bread) to make a full complement of amino acids. The general rule of thumb is to have grains and pulses or nuts and grains together.

## 4. (slightly) up your protein intake

Regular exercisers need more protein than inactive people. If you work out three or more days a week you need between 1.2 and 1.8 g of protein per kg of bodyweight daily. So, if you weigh 70 kg, you'll need 84–126 g of protein daily. That works out around 20–25% of your calorie intake (if you're keen on percentages!). Skimping on protein can cause fatigue and slow recovery after workouts. And lets face it, you can't build a building without adequate raw materials. It's pretty much the same when it comes to muscle growth – without enough protein, you won't be able to build a lean strong body.

## 5. be fat friendly

To get the most out of the fat you eat, make sure you get it from the right sources. Aim for most of your fat to be the monounsaturated and poly-unsaturated kind (see page 17), while avoiding saturated fats (see page 16) as far as possible.

Just what are the healthiest fats? There are two types of unsaturated fats – the omega-3 and omega-6 fatty acids – that are crucial for good health and immunity. They lower blood cholesterol levels and thus lower the risk of heart disease. A lack of either one will result in dry scaly skin. These fats are particularly beneficial for regular exercisers, because they can help you train smarter and get leaner. Researchers have shown that omega-3s increases the delivery of oxygen to exercising muscles, optimising your aerobic capacity, increasing your endurance and, ultimately, helping burn more body fat. They also help speed recovery after hard training and reduce inflammation and joint stiffness.

**PHYTONUTRIENTS**
Phytochemicals are compounds found naturally in plants. Many are powerful antioxidants that work with vitamins and minerals to protect the body from degenerative diseases (such as heart disease and cancer), boost immunity and fight harmful bacteria and viruses. There are hundreds of different types of phytochemicals and the best way to make sure you get enough of them is to eat at least five daily portions of fruits and vegetables.

## 6. get plenty of vitamins and minerals

Vitamins support the immune system, help the brain function properly and help convert food into energy. They are important for healthy skin and hair, controlling growth and balancing hormones. Some vitamins – the B vitamins and vitamin C – must be provided by the diet each day, as they cannot be stored.

Minerals are needed for structural and regulatory func-tions, including bone strength, haemoglobin manufacture, fluid balance and muscle contraction (see the Essential Vitamin and Mineral Guide, pages 78-82).

## 7. get a drinking habit

Make a habit of drinking regularly. Have a glass of water first thing in the morning and have frequent drink breaks during your day. Aim for 6–8 glasses (1–1½l) daily, and more in hot weather or when you exercise (see pages 30, 36 and 45). It's better to drink little and often rather than swigging large amounts in one go, which promotes urination and a greater loss of fluid.

## FATS EXPLAINED

*Saturated fats* are found in animal fats as well as products made with palm oil or palm kernel oil (a highly saturated fat). They have no beneficial role in keeping the body healthy – they raise blood cholesterol levels and increase the risk of heart disease – so we do not need any in the diet at all. Recognising that it would be impractical to cut out altogether, the UK Department of Health recommends that no more than 10% of total calories comes from saturated fat, equivalent to 10–20 g a day. The 2002 US National Academies of Science Institute of Medicine report states that there is no dietary requirement for saturated fat and advises keeping our intake as low as possible.

- fatty meats
- full-fat dairy products
- butter
- lard, shortening, dripping
- palm oil and palm kernel oil
- margarine, spreads, biscuits, cakes, desserts, etc made with palm or palm kernel oil
- egg yolk

*Trans fats* are even more harmful than *saturated fats*. They are formed during the commercial process of hydrogenation when liquid or vegetable oils are converted into hardened *hydrogenated fats*. There is no level of trans fatty acids that is safe according to the US Institute of Medicine, who recommends that we should aim for zero. These fats increase blood levels of LDL cholesterol ('bad' cholesterol) while lowering HDL ('good') cholesterol, pushing up your heart disease risk. Check food labels for *hydrogenated fats* and *partially hydrogenated fats*.

- margarine and low fat spread
- pastries, pies and tarts
- biscuits
- cereal bars, breakfast bars
- cakes and bakery products
- crackers
- ice cream desserts and puddings
- bought fried food

**Monounsaturated fats** actually lower harmful cholesterol levels and can cut your heart disease and cancer risk. The Department of Health recommends an intake of around 12% of total calories.

- olive oil and olive oil margarine
- rapeseed oil
- avocados
- soya oil
- peanuts, almonds, cashews
- peanut butter
- sunflower and sesame seeds
- mayonnaise

**Polyunsaturated fats**, in moderation, also reduce heart disease risk though less effectively than monounsaturated fats. The Department of Health recommends a maximum intake of 10% of total calories.

- sunflower, corn oil and safflower oil
- sunflower oil margarine
- nuts and seeds

**Omega-3 fatty acids** include alpha linolenic acid, eicosapentanoic acid (EPA) and docosahexanoic acid (DHA). You need only tiny amounts to keep you healthy but, as they are found in relatively few foods, many people struggle to meet the minimum requirement of 0.9 g a day. For heart disease prevention and good performance, aim to eat a minimum of 300 g (1–2 portions) of oily fish a week, or 1 tablespoon of an omega-3 rich oil daily.

- sardines
- mackerel
- salmon
- fresh (not tinned) tuna
- trout
- herring
- walnuts and walnut oil
- pumpkin seeds and pumpkinseed oil
- flax seeds and flaxseed oil
- rapeseed oil
- soya oil
- sweet potatoes
- omega-3 enriched eggs and margarine

**Omega-6 fatty acids** include linoleic acid and gamma linolenic acid (GLA), and are easier to find in foods than omega-3s. For this reason, most people currently eat too much omaga-6 in relation to omega-3, which results in an imbalance of prostaglandins ('mini hormones' responsible for controlling blood clotting, inflammation and the immune system). The average diet contains a ratio of 10:1. Aim for a ratio of no more than five times the amount of omega-6 to omega-3.

- sunflower oil, safflower oil, corn and groundnut oil
- sunflower oil margarine
- olive oil
- peanuts and peanut butter
- evening primrose oil
- sunflower and sesame seeds

# blueberry muffins

*This recipe is a delicious way of adding antioxidant-rich blueberries to your diet. These muffins are lower in fat than ordinary muffins – providing mostly healthy monounsaturated fats – higher in fibre and rich in vitamins. Try them after a workout to refuel your energy stores.*

**makes 12 muffins**
125 g (4 oz) self raising white flour
125 g (4 oz) self raising wholemeal flour
Pinch of salt
60 g (2 oz) sugar
3 tablespoons (45 ml) rapeseed or
    sunflower oil
1 egg
250 ml (8 fl oz) apple puree
1 teaspoon (5 ml) vanilla extract
200 ml (7 fl oz) skimmed milk
125 g (4 oz) fresh blueberries
    (or 85 g/3 oz dried blueberries)

- Pre-heat the oven to 200°C/400°F/Gas mark 6. Line 12 muffin tins with paper muffin cases or oil the tins well.

- In a bowl, mix together the flours, salt and sugar.

- In a separate bowl, mix together the oil, egg, apple puree, vanilla and milk then pour into the flour mixture. Stir until just combined.

- Gently fold in the blueberries.

- Spoon the mixture into the prepared muffin tins – about two-thirds full – and then bake for about 20 minutes until the muffins are risen and golden.

**TOP SCORING ANTIOXIDANT FRUIT AND VEGETABLES**

The table below shows the healthiest fruit and vegetables compiled by researchers at Tuft's University in Boston, US. Each fruit and vegetable was tested for its ability to combat harmful free radicals. ORAC stands for Oxygen Radical Absorbance Capacity, which calculates the ability of foods to soak up the free radicals. All of the foods in the table will significantly raise the antioxidant levels in your blood although the foods at the top will have a greater effect than those at the bottom. The ORAC values of prunes and raisins appear higher because these foods contain no water.

| Fruit | ORAC score | Vegetable | ORAC score |
|---|---|---|---|
| Prunes | 5,770 | Kale | 1,770 |
| Raisins | 2,830 | Spinach | 1,260 |
| Blueberries | 2,400 | Brussels sprouts | 980 |
| Blackberries | 2,036 | Alfalfa sprouts | 930 |
| Strawberries | 1,540 | Broccoli | 890 |
| Raspberries | 1,220 | Beets | 840 |
| Plums | 949 | Red peppers | 710 |
| Oranges | 750 | Onions | 450 |
| Red grapes | 739 | Corn | 400 |
| Cherries | 670 | Aubergines | 390 |
| Kiwi fruit | 602 | | |
| Pink grapefruit | 483 | | |

The ORAC (oxygen radical absorbance capacity) score is a measure of the total antioxidant power of a food.

Source: Human Nutrition Research Centre on Ageing, Tufts University, Boston, US.

# 8. eat your greens ... and reds, purples, yellows and oranges

*Mix your colours!*

There are hundred of phytonutrients in fruit and vegetables, each providing a different benefit to your body. Choosing foods from each colour category will ensure you get a wide range of phytonutrients and great health protection:

- green – watercress, broccoli, cabbage, rocket, Brussels sprouts, salad leaves, curly kale
- red/purple – plums, aubergines, cherries, beetroot, red grapes, strawberries, blackberries, blueberries, tomatoes
- yellow/orange – peaches, apricots, nectarines, oranges, yellow peppers, squash
- white/yellow – onions, garlic, apples, pears, celery
- brown/green – beans, lentils, bean sprouts, nuts, seeds, tea.

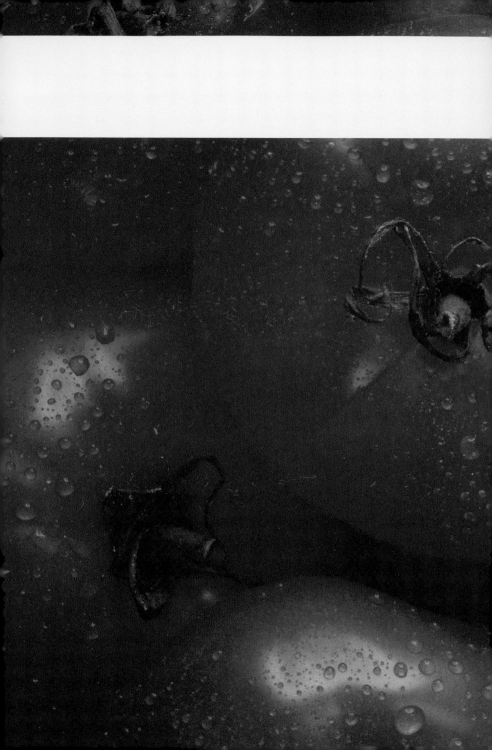

# before training

Do you often feel tired and 'heavy' during training? Have you ever found yourself flaking out half way through your workout? Do you often wonder how your mate manages to train a lot harder or a lot longer than you?

If you find yourself nodding wearily in agreement with these questions, you may have been eating the wrong foods before your workouts. You may unknowingly be suffering from mild dehydration or perhaps eating too soon before your workout. What and when you eat in relation to your workout makes a big difference to your energy, your performance and how much body fat you burn. If you want to get the best results from your training programme you need to make sure that you aren't leaving your eating and drinking to chance.

## fuelling for training

What you eat the day before and during the several hours before your workout dictates how much energy you will have for your next workout and how well you will perform. The carbohydrates in your food are converted into glycogen and stored in your muscles. Rather like filling your car up with petrol before a journey, you need to ensure your muscles are well fuelled before working out. In general, regular exercisers need around 4–7 g of carbohydrate for each kg of their body weight. Serious athletes who train for several hours a day may need as much as 10 g/kg. Table 2.1 tells you roughly how much carbohydrate you need according to your activity level. For example, if you weigh 65 kg and work out 3–5 hours a week, you should aim for 260–325 g of carbohydrate daily. Table 1.1 (page 10) gives the carbohydrate content of various foods to help you check your diet.

## 2.1 how much carbohydrate?

| activity level | g carbohydrate/kg/day |
|---|---|
| 3–5 hours/week | 4–5 |
| 5–7 hours/week | 5–6 |
| 1–2 hours/day | 6–7 |
| 2–4 hours/day | 7–8 |
| More than 4 hours/day | 8–10 |

### how can I tell if I'm eating too little or too much carbohydrate?

A good guide to whether you are eating enough is how energetic you feel during your workouts. Eating too little carbohydrate makes you feel fatigued, lethargic and kind of 'empty' during exercise – a bit like a car chugging along with very little petrol. Upping your carbohydrate intake – say an extra 50–100 g daily – should boost your energy levels, increase your endurance and up your speed. On the other hand, over-eating carbohydrates won't increase your energy levels further. Instead, you may feel 'heavy' and, ironically, more lethargic. It's a matter of listening to your own body and getting the balance right between too little and too much carbohydrate.

# eating just before training

What you eat just before exercise won't affect your muscle glycogen levels. Rather, it will increase your blood sugar levels, giving you more energy for training and possibly increasing your endurance.

## so when is the best time to eat?

Ideally, you should aim to have a meal between 2 and 4 hours before a workout. That should leave enough time to partially digest your food.

You should feel comfortable – not full and not hungry.

According to a study at the University of North Carolina in the US, eating a moderately-high carbohydrate, low fat meal 3 hours before exercise allows you to exercise longer and perform better. Researchers asked the athletes to run on treadmills, at a moderate intensity for 30 minutes with high intensity 30s intervals and then until they couldn't run any longer, after eating a meal either 6 hours or 3 hours beforehand. The athletes ran significantly longer after they had eaten the meal 3 hours before training compared with 6 hours.

> I advise my clients in the gym to try and eat 2–3 hours before a workout, preferably something that contains complex carbohydrates, such as pasta or a bowl of cereal. This gives them more energy to fuel their workout.
>
> KESH PATEL, EXERCISE SPECIALIST

Don't eat a big meal just before a workout otherwise you will feel uncomfortable and 'heavy', with little energy for training. And don't attempt to train on empty either. It's a myth that starving yourself before exercise makes you burn more fat. You wouldn't take your car out on a long journey when the petrol tank is low, so you can't expect to exercise very hard or very long when you haven't fuelled your body for several hours.

Here are five good reasons to eat a meal or snack 2–4 hours before working out:

## 1. to keep the shakes at bay

Train on empty and you may become light headed, weak and shaky. These are signs of low blood sugar levels and will certainly stop you from working out. When your brain isn't getting enough fuel, you'll feel faint, lose concentration and risk injury.

## 2. to keep going longer

Training on a full fuel (glycogen) tank with steady blood sugar levels will allow you to train longer and harder. Training on an empty stomach results in early fatigue. Rather like a car running out of petrol, your body will come to a weary halt.

## 3. to burn more body fat

Don't think that training on empty will force your body to dip into its fat reserves. Instead, working out with low blood sugar levels will almost certainly result in early fatigue. You'll have to reduce your intensity and/or stop early. So you'll end up burning fewer calories and less fat. Worse, your body turns to muscle protein when it doesn't have enough carbohydrate to burn. So you could end up losing hard-earned muscle instead of fat!

## 4. to keep up with your mates

Fuelling your body properly beforehand means that you will have more energy to burn. If you attempt to train on an empty fuel tank, you'll be the one at the back of the pack struggling to keep up with the pace.

## 5. to get you to the gym

When you haven't eaten for several hours you feel lethargic and unmotivated. It's hard to psyche yourself up to do anything in that state, let alone have a workout. So eating a light snack a couple of hours before your scheduled workout time will reduce the temptation to skip your workout.

---

**I prefer to work out first thing in the morning. Should I eat anything before my workout?**

This depends how much time you have between waking up and working out. If you wake up a couple of hours beforehand, you will have time to have a light breakfast or snack, such as some cereal, toast, fruit, yoghurt or an energy bar. Drink at least 300 ml of water or diluted juice before your morning workout. This helps to rehydrate you after your night's fast.

If you plan to work out almost immediately after waking up, you may not feel like eating solid food. And eating too soon before exercise may give you a stitch. Try having a drink – water, diluted fruit juice or even a small meal replacement shake (see page 88) to reduce the risk of dehydration during your workout. If you cannot eat anything at all, make sure that you eat plenty the day before and for breakfast after your workout.

# what are the best foods to eat just before a workout?

Slow-burning or low glycaemic foods – that is foods that produce a gradual rise in blood sugar levels (see page 9) – are the safest bet before working out. Studies at the University of Sydney have found that athletes who eat a low-glycaemic meal before exercise are able to keep going considerably longer than those who eat a high-glycaemic meal. It seems that low-glycaemic meals help spare muscle glycogen and avoid problems of low blood sugar levels during long training sessions.

Remember that you can make a low glycaemic meal either by eating carbohydrate foods with a low glycaemic index (such as apples, oranges, milk, beans) or by combining your carbohydrate source with protein and/or fat (see page 13). The boxes below give you some suggestions for pre-exercise snacks and meals.

---

**Will eating chocolate or a few sweets before training give me a quick energy fix?**

If your last meal was more than 4 hours ago, a small quantity of high-glycaemic carbs – equivalent to half a bar (25g) of chocolate – eaten just before training may help to give you an energy boost. You need to eat just enough to raise your blood sugar levels but not too much to cause a surge of insulin that would otherwise cause a sudden blood sugar fall. Also you need to get the timing right. Try eating something 15–30 minutes before training. Leaving too long a gap may result in mild hypoglycaemia (low blood sugar) as insulin kicks in before you start exercise – and that's the last thing you want!

---

> With the rugby players, I ensure their pre-match meal is high in carbohydrate and protein and low in fat. Peppers stuffed with rice, beans on toast with poached eggs and fruit are all favourites. Fatty foods are avoided like the plague!

CLIVE BREWER, SPORTS SCIENTIST AND ADVISOR TO THE RUGBY LIONS

## pre-workout meals

2–4 hours before exercise:

- sandwich/roll/bagel/wrap filled with chicken, fish, cheese, egg or peanut butter
- jacket potato with beans, cheese, tuna, coleslaw or chicken
- pasta with tomato-based pasta sauce and cheese
- macaroni cheese (with salad)
- rice or other grains with chicken or fish and vegetables
- porridge made with milk
- wholegrain cereal (e.g. bran or wheat flakes, muesli or Weetabix) with milk or yoghurt
- fish pie (fish in sauce with mashed potatoes)
- lean beef chilli (or vegetarian chilli) with rice
- noodles with stir-fried prawns (or tofu) and vegetables

## pre-workout snacks

1–2 hours before exercise:

- fresh fruit
- dried apricots or sultanas
- smoothie (home made or ready-bought)
- yoghurt
- shake (homemade or a meal replacement shake see page 88)
- energy or nutrition bar (see pages 85 and 89)
- cereal bar or breakfast bar
- fruit loaf or raisin bread
- banana cake (see recipe on page 29)
- diluted fruit juice

## WHAT SHOULD I EAT BEFORE A COMPETITION?

It's a good idea to take your own supplies of food and drink as suitable foods may not be available at the venue. Keep to the guidelines for training outlined above but it's worth remembering that competition nerves may take away your appetite or make it more difficult to digest your normal meals. In general:

- stick to familiar foods – don't try anything new
- be certain that what you're eating and drinking is un-contaminated and safe
- drink plenty of water
- avoid high-fat, salty or very sugary foods
- eat little and often (see the suggestions for pre-workout snacks on page 28)
- liquid meals such as shakes, smoothies and juices may be more palatable than solid food.

# easy banana cake

### makes 12 small cakes

85 g (3oz) soft brown sugar          125 ml (4 fl oz) skimmed milk
85 g (3oz) butter or margarine       200 g (7oz) self-raising flour
2 ripe bananas, mashed               Pinch of salt
1 egg                                ½ tsp (2.5 ml) nutmeg

- Preheat the oven to 190°C/375°F/Gas mark 5.
- Lightly butter or oil 12 muffin tins or line with 12 paper muffin cases.
- In a bowl, mix together the sugar and butter or margarine. Mix in the mashed bananas. Beat in the egg and milk.
- Fold in the flour, salt and nutmeg.
- Spoon into the prepared muffin tin and bake for about 20 minutes or until golden brown and firm to the touch.

# drinking before training

Make sure that you are properly hydrated before you start training. If you start exercising when you are mildly dehydrated and continue losing fluid, you will fatigue very quickly. Hydration helps to keep your body temperature stable so if you become dehydrated during exercise your body will overheat and you'll be unable to carry on exercising properly. The dangers of dehydration during exercise are explained in Chapter 3 (see pages 36–40).

Here are some guidelines on keeping hydrated before training:

## don't go for gold
Watching your urine is the best way to check your body's hydration. Dark gold coloured urine is a sure sign that you're low on fluid. Drink plenty of water and aim for light-yellow coloured urine.

## beat your thirst
Drink before you get thirsty. By the time your thirst mechanism kicks in you will have lost around 2% of your body weight as water. If you relied on your thirst alone, you would replace only 50–75% of what you need.

## drink early
Drink at least 2 glasses of water (400–600 ml) 2–3 hours before you workout. This is the amount recommended by the American college of Sports Medicine.

## be a bottle baby
Carry a bottle of water with you everywhere. To the gym, to the office, in the car. It'll be a constant reminder to drink. It need not be expensive bottled water. A simple water bottle or a bottled-water bottle will do – just refill with tap water.

## get into the drinking habit
Make a habit of drinking regularly. Have a glass of water first thing in the morning and then schedule drink stops during your day. Aim for at least 8 glasses (1½–2 l) daily, and more in hot weather or on workout days. It's better to drink little and often rather than swigging large amounts in one go, which promotes urination and a greater loss of fluid.

## DO COFFEE AND TEA COUNT?

Not all of your daily fluid needs to be in the form of water. US researchers at Dartmouth Medical School say even caffeine-containing drinks such as tea and coffee can count toward your daily fluid intake. Caffeine is a mild diuretic, but does not dehydrate the body as was once imagined. You can count a cup of weak tea as a cup of fluid and a cup of coffee as about half that volume.

## super-charge

*This drink is excellent for boosting your energy and vitality. The natural fruit sugars help to balance your blood sugar levels and provide your body with fuel. It is also a great source of vitamin C, beta-carotene, potassium and magnesium.*

**makes 400 ml (⅔ pint)**    ¼ pineapple (about 200 g/7 oz flesh)
¼ Galia melon (about 200 g/7 oz flesh)
1 pink grapefruit
Handful of seedless green grapes
A few ice cubes

You'll need a juicer for this recipe. Peel the pineapple, melon and grapefruit and divide into manageable-sized pieces. Juice the fruit then pour into a glass. Add a few ice cubes.

### Note on Juicing

*If you are serious about juicing it is worth investing in the best machine that you can afford. Choose a juicer with a reputable brand name, that has an opening big enough for larger fruit and vegetables, and make sure that it is easy to clean. Prepare the ingredients for juicing just before juicing so they won't lose their vitamins. Cut fruit and vegetables into manageable pieces. You can put most parts of the produce into the juicer, except hard skins (e.g. citrus peel, banana peel, etc) and stones (e.g. from avocados, peaches, apricots, etc.).*

# during training

For most activities lasting less than an hour, knocking back anything other than water is unnecessary. But if you are planning to exercise for longer – a half-marathon, a mini-triathlon or long bike ride – you will need to learn to eat and drink on the run. That may sound pretty tricky but doing so could just give you the edge. Taking in plenty of fluid and extra carbohydrate (in the form of a drink or as solid food) will almost certainly help you to keep going longer.

If you work out for less than an hour, you will need to keep a water bottle handy and make sure that you drink the right amount at the right times.

## eating

Studies have shown that consuming some kind of carbohydrate during a workout lasting longer than 60 minutes can help you keep going longer. This carbohydrate helps to keep your blood sugar levels steady and fuels your muscles, particularly in the latter stages of your workout when glycogen reserves are likely to be low. It won't get converted into glycogen but it will help your muscles to keep exercising longer.

### how much carbohydrate?

Researchers at the University of Texas in Austin recommend 30–60 g of carbohydrate for each hour of exercise. That's equivalent to about 120–240 calories per hour. Any more than that won't give you any further benefit as the muscles can't take up more than 60 g of glucose per hour from the bloodstream. Here are some tips for eating on the run:

### *start eating early*

Start consuming carbohydrate early in your workout, ideally in the first 30 minutes. It takes at least 30 minutes for the carbohydrate to reach your muscles so don't wait for an hour or until you feel tired before you begin eating and drinking.

### eat little and often
Your goal is to maintain a steady supply of carbohydrate entering your bloodstream. Aim to consume 15–30 g every 30 minutes.

### go for the fast-burn
Choose fast-burning carbohydrates – drinks and foods with a high or moderate glycaemic index (see page 10) as you need to get the carbohydrate into your bloodstream rapidly. Sugar, glucose and maltodextrin (glucose polymers) would be suitable but cereal products (bars, biscuits) work equally well. Choose products containing less than 5 g fat per portion.

### skip the carbs for fat burning
If you're trying to lose fat, don't have extra carbs during your workout. Steering clear of carbs immediately before and during training keeps insulin levels low and so encourages your muscles to burn slightly more fat as fuel. Have your meal about 4 hours before training. This strategy works best for workouts lasting less than one hour – after that time you'll be running low on energy and won't be able to keep up your usual pace. You'll also risk burning muscle as your muscles turn to protein as a fuel when glycogen and blood sugar levels fall.

## what should I eat?
Your choice will really depend on your activity or sport. Drinks containing some kind of carbohydrate are the most practical option for most people as you get fluid at the same time. If you decide to go for solid food – say on a cycle ride or hike – it needs to be portable, palatable, non-perishable and very easy to eat. Experiment to find the best drinks and foods for you. The box on the next page gives some suggestions for easy workout foods (see also Chapter 8–11).

## workout foods (when training for longer than 60 minutes)

- energy bar
- cereal or breakfast bar
- energy gel
- raisins or sultanas
- bananas
- biscuits (low fat)

Have these with plenty of water. The sizes of bars, gels and biscuits vary enormously. Check the carbohydrate content on the label to work out how much you'll need to supply 30–60 g per hour. Choose products that supply less than 5 g fat per portion.

### CARB UP FOR BETTER IMMUNITY

Does intense training often leave you susceptible to colds and infections? It's ironic that moderate training boosts your immune system but hard training can lower your defences against germs and viruses – especially when combined with poor eating habits. The reason? Heavy prolonged training results in increased levels of stress hormones (e.g. adrenaline and cortisol), which inhibits your immune system. But don't despair! Researchers from the University of Birmingham suggest the following:

- make sure you eat enough calories to match your needs – remember to eat more on the days you train
- ensure you're consuming plenty of foods rich in immunity-boosting nutrients – vitamins A, C, and E, vitamin $B_6$, zinc, iron and magnesium. The best sources are fresh fruit, vegetables, whole grains, beans, lentils, nuts and seeds.
- a modest antioxidant supplement may help to boost your defences and reduce the risk of upper respiratory infections (see also page 121). Avoid mega-doses

- avoid training in a carbohydrate-depleted state, e.g. following a low carbohydrate diet. Low glycogen stores are associated with bigger increases in cortisol levels and a bigger suppression of your immune cells
- during long tough workouts, consume 30–60 g of carbohydrate per hour to stave off the rise in stress hormones and the associated drop in immunity
- drink plenty of fluid. This increases your saliva production, which contains anti-bacterial proteins that can fight off air-borne germs
- try taking supplements of *echinacea* for up to 4 weeks during a period of hard training. Studies with athletes and non-athletes have shown that this herbal supplement boosts the body's own production of immune cells and results in greater protection against minor illnesses.

# drinking

As soon as you begin exercising, you lose water in the form of sweat. Sweating is actually a very good thing as it rids your body of the excess heat produced in your muscles. If this didn't happen you would quickly over-heat and die. You can lose about 500 ml in 30 minutes, depending on the heat, humidity and exercise intensity.

If you don't replace that water, your core temperature will rise and your performance will suffer. As your blood becomes 'thicker', your heart needs to beat faster to pump the blood around your body, and your body is put under undue stress.

**WATER THOSE MUSCLES**

Dehydration not only reduces your endurances but saps your strength too. Researchers at the Old Dominion University in Virginia, USA, tested the strength of ten young weight trainers on the bench press following dehydration. The amount of weight they could lift was significantly lower (by about 6 kg or 13 lbs) when they were dehydrated compared to when they were rehydrated. So water those muscles and watch them grow!

Losing the equivalent of 2% of your body weight as sweat – that's a mere 1.3 kg loss if you weigh 65 kg – results in a 10–20% drop in your performance (or aerobic capacity). Whatever kind of exercise you are doing, once you become mildly dehydrated it will be harder to keep going at the same intensity. And you will be forced to drop your pace.

## how much should I drink?

During exercise you should aim to match your fluid loss with your intake. Studies with athletes at the University of Aberdeen have shown that if you can replace at least 80% of your fluid loss or keep within 1% of your body weight, then your performance won't be affected. Exactly how much you need to drink depends on how heavily you are sweating.

The harder and longer you are working out, the more you sweat. Training in hot humid conditions also makes you sweat more. And some people simply sweat more than others.

In general, you can count on losing around 750–1000 ml per hour so you'll need to put back around 600– 800 ml in that time. Now that may sound like a tall order – particularly if you are out running or playing a team sport – but it can be done. You'll need to schedule in drink breaks and learn to drink on the run. If you can only manage a few sips at a time, then make sure you do that frequently, say every 10 minutes. Chapters 8–11 give some practical tips on managing drinking and eating while exercising.

**The most important thing that affected my performance was drinking water. I would drink 1 litre before training in the morning then continue drinking water during the session. If I didn't drink enough during and after training, I would feel really tired during my next training session. Like my other team members, I always weighed myself before and after training to calculate my fluid losses.**

TOM UPSHER, EX-PROFESSIONAL
FOOTBALL PLAYER, FULHAM FC

The American College of Sports Medicine and American Dietetics Association recommends drinking around 150–350 ml every 15–20 minutes. You should start drinking early during your workout as it takes about 30 minutes for the fluid to be absorbed into your bloodstream.

**Don't wait until you feel thirsty as this indicates that you are already on your way to dehydration!**

## working out how much to drink

To work out how much fluid you lose in a typical workout and, therefore, how much you ought to drink, weigh yourself before and after exercising. You can assume that all of your weight loss is fluid. A weight loss of ½ kg represents a fluid loss of 500 ml. So if you have lost ½ kg, that indicates a loss of 500 ml fluid. Aim to replace that fluid loss with 1½ times that volume of fluid.

This accounts for the fact that you continue sweating after exercise (and losing fluid) and that urination is usually increased during this time. So, if you have lost 0.5 kg, you should aim to drink 750 ml (0.75 kg) of fluid during and after your workout. Divide this volume into manageable amounts, according to the activity you are doing. For example, you could drink 125 ml (about half a cup) four times during your workout, and a further 250 ml immediately after your workout.

## case study

Keely, 29, is a successful middle distance runner. Her biggest problem was not being able to drink during training without feeling sick and, as it turned out, under-drinking the rest of the day. I suggested that she first worked on drinking regularly during the day. This would make sure that she was properly hydrated before training. Once she got used to drinking more generally, I asked her to practice taking frequent sips during training. She had a target amount in her water bottle, which was initially quite small then gradually increased over a couple of weeks. I encouraged her to try different drinks – water, diluted juice, squash, sports drinks – and different flavours. She found that water and very dilute apple juice (1 part juice to 2 parts water) suited her, but anything more concentrated sat in her stomach longer and made her feel sick. Within two months, Keely had worked out a drinking strategy that suited her sport, she felt less tired at the end of her workouts and noticed faster recovery between workouts.

# what should I drink?

## *workouts lasting less than one hour*

For most activities, water is all you need. It is absorbed relatively fast into your bloodstream so does a very good job at keeping your body hydrated. It's cheap, plentiful and readily available. If you're not keen on the taste and cannot force enough down, flavour it with a little cordial, fruit juice or high-juice squash. Obviously, any kind of squash or juice contributes extra sugar (carbohydrate) but, provided it's well diluted, this won't harm your performance. Sugar-free drinks are bit of an additive nightmare but, if you like the taste, it's better that you drink these than nothing.

> Many of the rugby players I advise drink a diluted sports drink, made up weaker than the manufacturer's instructions as they find the 'full strength' version tastes too strong and sweet. Other players do not like isotonic drinks – they complain that it feels too sticky in the mouth – so they drink plain water during a game.
>
> CLIVE BREWER, SPORTS SCIENTIST AND ADVISOR TO THE RUGBY LIONS

## *workouts lasting more than one hour*

Drinks containing carbohydrates – sports drinks, diluted juice and high-juice squash – are often a better choice than plain water when you are working out continually for longer than 60 minutes. The sugars they contain not only provide fuel for your exercising muscles but they also speed up the absorption of water into your bloodstream. And that counts when you're sweating heavily.

Ideally, you should aim to consume 30–60 g of carbohydrate per hour. That's equivalent to 500 ml–1 litre of an isotonic sports drink (containing 6 g sugar per 100 ml) or fruit juice diluted 50/50 with water. Start drinking early in your workout as it takes about 30 minutes for the water and sugars to reach your bloodstream.

> During the breaks between fights, I swig a sports drink to replace my fluid loss and keep my glucose levels topped up throughout the day's competition.
>
> GRAHAM CLAYTON, BRITISH FENCING TEAM 1994–2002

## summer berry quencher

*Packed with vitamin C, potassium and antioxidants, this delicious juice is a terrific way of getting all the goodness of summer fruits. It'll re-energise you during or after a long workout.*

**makes 200 ml (7 fl oz)**   1 kiwi fruit
6 strawberries
60 g (2 oz) raspberries
175 g (6 oz) pineapple (fresh
   or tinned)
A few ice cubes

You'll need a juice extractor for this recipe. Peel the kiwi fruit. Cut the pineapple into manageable sized pieces. Juice the fruit. Pour into a glass then add a few ice cubes.

*See note on juicing and juicers, page 31*

## performance or fat loss?

If you are aiming to lose body fat, drink plain water during your workout. Sports drinks add extra calories and in some cases may even supply as many – or more – calories as you are burning off!

However, if your main aim is to improve your fitness, strength or performance and you are working out longer than one hour, then a sports drink will help you to keep going longer. Research from the University of Texas found that drinking water during one hour of cycling improved performance by 6% compared with no water, but drinking a sports drink resulted in a 12% improvement on performance.

## could I drink too much water?

It is possible, though not common, to over-hydrate. There is a condition called *hyponatraemia* or 'water intoxication', which is caused by drinking too much water. This can happen during events lasting several hours – such as cycling, marathon running and hiking – when you sweat a lot, and drink water all the time. Excessive sweating combined with drinking only water dilutes the concentration of salts in the body to a dangerous level. The result is nausea, lethargy, dizziness and mental confusion; it's possible to lapse into a coma. If you think that you might be suffering from hyponatraemia you should not drink plain water; instead drink a litre per hour of a drink containing sugar and salt, such as an isotonic sports drink or diluted juice/squash with a pinch of salt.

# 4 after training

After your workout, what happens next? You crawl back home to watch TV or you race to your next business meeting; but what should happen is that you begin refuelling your body with the right foods.

Amazingly, it's after – not during – your workout that your body gets stronger and fitter. That's the whole idea isn't it? Eat the wrong kinds of food and you'll feel exhausted for the rest of the day with little energy. You'll feel sore longer and your gains will be slow. On the other hand, eat the right foods and you'll have more energy, feel stronger and achieve faster fitness gains.

## five steps to recovery

### 1. replace fluids

You need to replace the fluid you have lost during exercise as soon as possible afterwards. Failure to do so can leave you feeling listless and with a headache. See page 38 to calculate how much you should drink. As a rule of thumb you need to drink 750 ml of water for every ½ kg (1 lb) of body weight lost during your workout. Drinking slowly rather than guzzling the lot in one go will hydrate you better.

### 2. replace electrolytes

Unless you have been sweating heavily, electrolyte (mineral salts) loss is less critical than water loss. These can be easily replaced by food eaten in your next normal meal. But if you have been exercising hard for longer than one hour and lost a lot of fluid through sweating, you may need to replace those electrolytes straight away with a sports drink. The sodium in sports drinks helps your body to retain the fluid better than plain water.

### 3. replace carbohydrate

Carbohydrate helps your muscles recover after exercise and provides the fuel needed for your next workout. It is converted into glycogen one and a half times faster than normal during the 2 hours after training. If you workout daily, speedy recovery is crucial so have a carbo drink or snack (see below) as soon as possible after your workout, ideally no later than 30 minutes afterwards. If you intersperse your workouts with a rest day or two, aim to have a light carbohydrate snack some time within 2 hours of training.

### 4. add protein

Your post-workout drink or snack should, ideally, include protein as well as carbo-hydrate. According to researchers at Texas State University in the US, eating a mixture of carbohydrate and protein speeds glycogen recovery faster than eating carbo-hydrate alone. They found that adding a little protein to post-workout carbs boosted glycogen storage by almost 40%. It also promoted faster muscle repair and growth in weight trainers.

> I take my own supply of snacks – rice cakes, low fat biscuits – and my own home-made sports drink to have after football training or after a match. When travelling back from a match, the whole team refuels on the coach with high-carbohydrate meals, such as lasagne and shepherd's pie

TOM UPSHER, EX-PROFESSIONAL
FOOTBALL PLAYER, FULHAM FC

Here's why — the combination of protein and carbs stimulates insulin release, which prompts the muscle cells to take up glucose and amino acids faster from the bloodstream.

### 5. get your antioxidants

Have you noticed how hard training sometimes leaves your muscles really sore afterwards? One of the factors responsible is a build up of free radicals (molecules that have one or more unpaired electrons in their orbit), which are generated during exercise. Unchecked, they can eventually lead to heart disease and cancer but, in the short-term, they can damage cell membranes and make your muscles sore. While regular exercise increases your body's natural defences against free radicals, you can boost them further by consuming plenty of foods rich in antioxidant nutrients. Antioxidants are found in fruits, vegetables, whole grains and pulses.

# what to drink after your workout

As soon as you've finished exercising, think drink before you even get showered and changed. Water, diluted juice and sports drinks are all good fluid replacers. For most fitness activities lasting an hour or less plain water is a good choice. But if you have been exercising hard for longer than an hour drinks that containing sugar or maltodextrin (carbohydrate) and sodium may speed your recovery. According to research at the University of Iowa, carbohydrate increases water absorption. They found that drinks containing approximately 6 g carbohydrate/100 ml (range 3–8g/100 ml) are absorbed the most rapidly.

Studies at Yale University found that sodium encourages water retention, stimulates thirst (so you drink more) reduces urine output and so rehydrates athletes better after training.

The bottom line is that you need to rehydrate after exercise and it's better that you have a drink that you like the taste of rather than struggling to drink one you don't like. Monitor your urine. Drink plenty of fluids until your urine is pale yellow.

## tropical smoothie

*This delicious post-workout drink will replenish your fluid losses and refuel your glycogen stores. It's also packed with vitamin C, beta-carotene and other powerful antioxidants that will help boost your immune system and fight the free radicals produced during intense exercise.*

**makes 2 drinks**
6 ice cubes
300 ml (½ pint) pineapple juice
2 kiwi fruit, peeled and chopped
1 ripe mango, peeled, stoned and chopped
Sprigs of mint (optional)

- Place the ice cubes in the goblet of a smoothie maker, blender or food processor and process until slushy.
- Add the pineapple juice, kiwi fruit, mango flesh and mint leaves and blend until smooth. Chill in the fridge or drink immediately.

# what to eat after your workout

Ironically, hard training can suppress your post-workout appetite. As more of your blood flow is concerned with your exercising muscles, the hunger signals from the gut sensors become weakened. So, the thought of eating straight after a workout may make you feel queasy. If that's the case liquid meals (see below) are often easier to manage.

The ideal post-exercise snack should contain carbohydrate and a little protein. A study at the University of Texas at Austin in the US, found that a ratio of about 3:1 works best. So, aim to consume about 3 g of carbs for every 1 g of protein. The box below gives suggestions for post-workout snacks and meals.

**REFUELLING SNACKS** (to be eaten within 2 hours after exercise)

**meal replacement shake**

Shakes made up with milk or water give you an easy and convenient mini-meal in a glass. Powders and ready-to-drink versions generally contain a balanced mixture of carbohydrate (usually as maltodextrins and sugar), protein (usually whey), vitamins and minerals.

**couple of pieces of fresh fruit with a drink of milk**

Fruit is a terrific natural source of antioxidants and easy to eat on the go. Make a habit of carrying a supply with you during the day so you're never far from a healthy snack.

**1 or 2 cartons of yoghurt**

Fruit yoghurt contains almost the ideal carbohydrate to protein ratio for post-workout refuelling. Bingo!

**smoothie (crushed fresh fruit whizzed in a blender)**

Create your own flavour combos according to what you have available but, in general, bananas, strawberries, pears, mango and pineapple give the best results. Try the 'tropical smoothie' on page 45.

**homemade milkshake**

Really a do-it-yourself version of a meal replacement shake. Use milk, yoghurt and fresh fruit (such as bananas and strawberries) for an excellent mixture of protein, carbs and those all important antioxidants.

**yoghurt drink**

Probiotic yoghurt drinks are the best choices as they're great for boosting immunity as well as supplying protein, calcium and carbs.

**sports bar**

Bars containing a mixture of carbohydrate and protein are really handy after workouts.

**tuna or cottage cheese sandwich**

Any kind of low-fat protein food together with some kind of (preferably wholemeal) bread – whether it's the sliced kind, rolls, bagels, pitta or wraps – makes a great refuelling snack.

**handful of dried fruit and nuts**

Dried fruit not only provides carbs but also vitamins, minerals, antioxidants and fibre. Although nuts contain fat it's the healthy unsaturated kind.

**few rice cakes with jam or cottage cheese**

Rice cakes are many gym-goer's favourites – easy to carry around and munch when you're on the go. Just add a little protein for a well-balanced post-workout snack.

**bowl of wholegrain cereal with milk**

Cereal and milk (or yoghurt) makes an easy breakfast after a morning workout.

**bowl of porridge made with milk**

Porridge is an ideal recovery food as it provides carbs, protein, B vitamins and fibre.

**jacket potato with tuna or cottage cheese**

Top your jacket potato with a low fat high-protein food – try tuna, cottage cheese, chicken or baked beans – and add a side salad.

**Be organised and prepare your food in advance if you know that you'll be pressed for time later on. I advise my rugby players to take tubs of rice or pasta salad with them and have small amounts throughout the day.**

CLIVE BREWER, SPORTS SCIENTIST AND STRENGTH & CONDITIONING SPECIALIST

## REFUELLING MEALS

Follow your post-workout snack or meal with moderate-carbo-hydrate moderate-protein low fat meals every 2–4 hours. Eating 4–6 regular small meals ensures a steady supply of fuel to your muscles and reduces the chances of fat storage. Eating most of your carbohydrate intake in the earlier part of the day (morning and afternoon) rather than the evening will help fuel your body and prevent fat gain.

## fruit buns

*Try these delicious fruit buns after a tough workout. They provide plenty of carbohydrate and fibre and are handy for eating on the go. You can add other kinds of dried fruit, too. Try dried apricots, mango pieces, apple or pineapple.*

**makes 12 servings**

125 g (4 oz) sugar
125 g (4 oz) butter or margarine
2 eggs
225 g (8 oz) self-raising flour
½ teaspoon (1.2 ml) ground mixed spice
Pinch of salt
90 ml (3 fl oz) milk
85 g (3 oz) raisins or sultanas

- Preheat the oven to 200°C/400°F/Gas mark 6. Lightly butter or oil 12 muffin tins or line with 12 paper muffin cases.
- Mix the sugar and butter or margarine together until smooth and creamy.
- Beat in the eggs then fold in the flour, mixed spice, salt, milk and dried fruit.
- Spoon the mixture into the prepared muffin tin. Bake for approx. 15 minutes or until golden brown and firm to the touch.

**I work out in the evening and often don't get home until 8 or 9 o'clock. Should I eat anything this late at night?**

Always eat and drink after your workout no matter how late it is. Your body needs carbohydrate, protein and other nutrients to recover after training. Skipping that post-workout meal will delay your recovery and leave you tired for your next workout. Provided you don't overeat, these calories will not be turned into fat.

But aim to consume most of your calories and nutrients during the early part of the day – have a good breakfast, lunch and 2 or 3 snacks in between meals, to ensure that you are properly fuelled before your evening workout. After working out, have a drink straight away then a light meal or snack. Try jacket potatoes with tuna or cottage cheese, pasta with a light sauce, or a chicken salad with rice, meal replacement shake or bar. Finally, make sure that you plan ahead and have all the right ingredients to hand to avoid the temptation of relying on fast foods, sugary snacks or ready meals.

# eating for fat loss

Whether you're trying to lose that last bit of fat covering your abs or you have several pounds to lose before reaching your ideal physique, the principles of fat loss are the same. Simply put, you need to eat less and workout more. But the reality is not as simple because there are so many factors that affect your food choices, appetite and exercise habits that it's hard to get the balance right. And there is so much conflicting advice, so many diet books, diet foods and supplements on the shelves, it's hard to know what really works. That's why this chapter is essential reading for everyone wanting to lose body fat. It gives you the proven facts on eating and exercise for fat loss, as well as realistic tips that work.

## don't be too strict

Going on a strict diet may cause the pounds to drop off but can make you feel lethargic and weak, hindering your efforts in the gym. Worse, your body can end up hoarding instead of burning fat. A sudden drop in calories tells your body to conserve energy, as starvation might be imminent. Your body goes into survival mode and the rate at which you burn energy slows down. Your body adapts to survive on a lower calorie intake, which means that when you stop dieting, you're likely to put the weight back on.

Also, to compensate for the low calorie intake, your body will start to break down muscle tissue for fuel. So, you

The most common mistake I see my clients make when embarking on a weight loss programme is not eating enough calories. They half-starve themselves and end up not having enough energy to get through their workout. It's important that you fuel your body properly even if you want to lose weight.

LEE MASON, PERSONAL TRAINER

can end up losing muscle as well as fat.

**The easiest way to lose fat and keep it off is regular exercise plus a healthy and careful calorie intake**.

## BODY FAT

You need some body fat to survive. Your brain needs it, your nerves need it, you need it in the marrow of your bones and you need it around your organs to cushion them and keep them warm. Women need a certain amount to maintain normal hormonal balance and menstrual function. All this accounts for about 3% (in men) or 9–12% (in women) of your body weight. The rest is stored under your skin – that's the fat that shows – and around your abdominal organs.

Scientists recommend body fat levels between 18–25% for women and 13–18% for men. These ranges are associated with the lowest health risk in population studies.

However, lower body fat levels are advantageous to performance in many sports and levels in the region of 10–18% in women and 5–10% in men are common among elite athletes.

# calories count

Calories do count! The only way to lose fat is to take in fewer calories than your body needs for basic functions and daily activities. Consume more calories than you need and your body will store them as fat. It's as simple as that.

How many calories make half a kilo (1 pound) of fat? The answer is about 3500 whether they are coming or going. If you eat 3500 more calories than you need, they will be stored and add half a kilo (1 lb) to your weight. On the other hand, burn 3500 more calories than you eat and you'll lose half a kilo (1 lb).

You're probably doing some training already so roughly 50–70% of that deficit should come from a calorie reduction, the remainder should come from increased exercise or daily activity.

Think of it like this. To lose half a kilo per week, you can reduce your calorie intake by 350 a day and step up your expenditure by 150 a day.

## what is a calorie?

Everyone talks about calories as if they are 'something' contained in food. In fact, a calorie is a scientific unit of heat measurement. One calorie is the amount of energy needed to raise the temperature of 1 g of water by 1°C. As this is a very small amount of energy, scientists tend to use a larger unit called a kilocalorie (kcal), which is the amount of energy need to raise the temperature of 1 kg of water by 1°C. This is equivalent to 1000 calories. The energy value of food is, strictly speaking measured in kcal (you will have seen this on food labels) but, to keep things simple, most people use the term calories when talking about food.

**WHAT IS A SAFE RATE OF FAT LOSS?**
Experts agree between half and one kilo (1–2 lb) per week is a healthy and effective rate of weight loss. A loss of more than one kilo (2 lb) per week means you could be losing muscle.

# what exactly is metabolism?

Metabolism is the sum total of all the chemical and physical processes by which the body converts the foods you eat into energy. The *metabolic rate* is the rate your body burns calories for energy. Your *basal metabolic rate* (BMR) is the rate at which you burn calories on basic body functions, such as breathing, blood circulation and maintaining a constant body temperature. It accounts for most of the calories you burn daily. As a rule of thumb, BMR uses 11 calories for every half-kilo (1 lb) of a woman's body weight and 12 calories per half kilo (1 lb) of a man's body weight. For example, a woman weighing 60 kg burns 1320 calories daily just to run her body. That's without moving or doing any kind of physical activity. A man weighing 75 kg burns 1800 calories.

However, your BMR also depends on the percentage of lean muscle tissue in your body. Muscle cells are up to eight times more metabolically active than fat cells so the more muscle you have, the higher your BMR.

## can you boost your metabolism?

The only safe and effective way to increase your metabolic rate is with exercise. The harder you work, the faster your metabolic rate. The metabolic increase continues after exercise as your body burns extra calories to replenish its energy reserves and repair muscle tissue. The longer and more intense the workout, the greater the 'after-burn'. Intense weights workouts may raise your metabolic rate for up to five hours; for less intense aerobic workouts the after burn may last less than an hour.

But to increase your metabolic rate in the long-term you have to increase your lean body tissue. Adding one kilo (2 lb) of muscle is estimated to burn an extra 65 calories a day. So the more muscle you have, the easier it becomes to stay lean!

## does your metabolism slow down as you get older?

Most people notice that their weight creeps up year by year even though their eating habits haven't changed. The likely explanation is that their metabolic rate has slowed. Unless you exercise regularly, you'll lose around 0.25 kg (½ lb) of muscle every year after your late twenties. And as you lose muscle, your body burns fewer calories. As a result, the BMR drops about 2 per cent each decade. Weight gain is compounded if people also cut back on the amount of activity they do. To maintain what you've got, you would have to increase your calorie expenditure 2 per cent or eat 2 per cent fewer calories. Suppose you needed 2500 calories when you were 30 but then didn't make any changes to your eating or exercise habits, that represents a 50 calorie excess each day. Over 365 days, that represents 18,250 excess calories or a weight gain of 2.6 kg (5 lbs).

Fortunately, you can combat age-related muscle loss with weight training. Just two sessions a week can make a big difference to your metabolism and your body.

# train smart for fat loss

For the best fat-burning results, the American College of Sports Medicine recommends two weight training sessions a week in addition to three 20–40 minute sessions of aerobic (cardiovascular) activity. You won't necessarily burn more calories lifting weights than doing aerobic exercise but the increased muscle mass you develop as a result will make your body burn more calories every day.

# build muscle

The most effective strategy for building – and toning – muscle and burning fat simultaneously is high-intensity weight training. This doesn't mean lifting heavy weights but, rather, working each body part with 2–4 sets with a weight you can lift only 8–12 times, taking 30 seconds rest between sets. See page 95 for more information on weight training.

# do aerobics

Aerobic activity not only burns excess calories but also increases your body's ability to burn fat.

Aim for 20–40 minutes per session, 3–5 times a week. But don't do too much. Studies have shown that after about 60–90 minutes of aerobic activity, the body begins to break down and use muscle tissue as fuel. And on a calorie-restricted diet, this happens earlier on in your workout. Lose muscle and your BMR slows so you won't burn as many calories.

Any kind of activity that uses the large muscle groups of the body and can be kept up for 20–40 minutes with your heart rate in your target training range (see page 59) counts. Try running, elliptical training machines, swimming, cycling, fast walking and group exercise classes. Mix and match your activities so you don't get bored. Remember that the higher the resistance, the more muscle you will build, so high-resistance activities such as rowing, stair-climbing, incline running and hard cycling are good for strengthening as well as defining muscles.

## calculating your target heart rate

The harder you work the more calories you'll use. As a guide you should be working at least 60 per cent of your maximum heart rate (MHR). Subtract your age in years from 220 multiplied by 0.6. But for fastest improvements in your fitness, try to work nearer to 85 per cent of your MHR.

For example, a 30 year-old bodybuilder working out between 60–85% of his MHR:

$$220 - 30 = 190$$
$$190 \times 0.6 = 114$$
$$190 \times 0.85 = 162$$

His target heart rate range is 114–162 beat per minute. Working lower than 114 is not efficient for conditioning his heart and lungs or fat burning, and working higher than 162 may reduce the effectiveness of the fat burning programme.

**Which type of workout boosts your metabolic rate the most: weights or aerobics?**

This question was the subject of a study at Colorado State University in the US. The researchers measured the post-exercise oxygen uptake (EPOC) and the metabolic rate (MR) in volunteers after completing an hour's intense weights workout or an hour's aerobics workout. Both workouts burned a similar number of calories. The researchers found that the weights workout increased the EPOC and metabolic rate considerably more than the aerobics workout, the biggest difference occurring during the first two hours after exercise. What's more the MR of those who completed the weights workout remained higher than normal 14 hours later. So, intense weights workouts are the best way to boost your metabolic rate and burn more calories in the long term.

# eating strategy

## step 1: get an idea of how many calories you should be eating

There are two ways of doing this:

**a** *Estimate your current calorie intake then cut by 15%*
This method works best for those who already have a fairly low calorie intake. Reducing calories by 15% will minimise the drop in your metabolic rate that normally accompanies a calorie drop. Record your food intake for seven days. Be as accurate as possible, recording the exact weights of all foods and drinks consumed. Use food tables, the internet or food labels to work out your daily calorie intake. Add up all seven days, then divide by seven to get a daily average. Then subtract 15% from that number (multiply by 0.85). This will be your new calorie intake to start losing fat.

## DO EARLY MORNING WORKOUTS ON AN EMPTY STOMACH BURN MORE FAT?

If fat loss is your goal, the best time to do aerobic exercise is first thing in the morning before eating when insulin levels are at their lowest and glucagon levels are at their highest. This encourages more fat to leave your fat cells and travel to your muscles, where the fat is burned. Of course, you won't burn more calories but more of the calories you do burn will come from fat. Over time, this may lead to speedier fat loss. But if performance is your goal, you will be better off eating 2–4 hours before exercise. The resulting rise in blood glucose levels slows the rate of glycogen depletion, enabling you to exercise harder and longer.

**b** *Calculate your calorie needs*
To give you a good idea of how many calories you should be eating, here is a quick formula to get a ballpark figure for your daily needs.

**1**: *Estimate your basal metabolic rate (BMR):*
    Women: BMR = weight in kgs × 2 × 11 (alternatively weight in lbs × 11)
    Men: BMR = weight in kgs × 2 × 12 (alternatively weight in lbs × 12)
(e.g. for 60 kg woman: BMR = 60 × 2 × 11 = 1320)

**2**: *Estimate your lifestyle activity level:*
Inactive or sedentary: BMR × 20%
Fairly active (include walking and exercise 1–2 × week): BMR × 30%
Moderately active (exercise 2–3 × weekly): BMR × 40%
Active (exercise hard more than 3 × weekly): BMR × 50%
Very active (exercise hard daily): BMR × 70%
(e.g. for moderately active 60 kg woman: 1320 × 40% = 528)

**3**: *Add the two together to work out your daily calorie needs*
(e.g. for moderately active 60 kg woman: 1320 + 528 = 1848)
That's how many calories you burn a day to maintain your weight, assuming you have an 'average' body composition. If you have higher than average muscle mass add 150 calories.

Remember you will lose half a kilo (1 lb) for every 3,500 calorie deficit. To lose weight, subtract 350 from that number and increase your calorie expenditure by 150 a day; this will produce a fat loss of about half a kilo (1 lb) per week; (see page 52).

## step 2: start keeping a food diary

Hardly eat a thing? Keeping a food diary will give you a much clearer idea of where your calories are coming from. Write down everything that passes your lips for three days (or longer if you can manage it), noting the portion weights and sizes. Try to be as accurate as possible, recording the weights of everything and remembering to write down every snack and every drink. Be as honest as possible – that handful of crisps, those biscuits while making tea, that pint of beer after work. You may be surprised how quickly the calories add up or how often you nibble. Now put your eating habits to the test by comparing your portions with the recommendations of the Fitness Food Pyramid.

## step 3: recognise the culprit foods

Look at your food diary and identify the foods or drinks that really aren't helping your fat loss efforts. Work out which types of food you need to reduce or increase.

Clearly fat is more 'fattening' than protein or carbohydrate so it makes sense to cut fats to 15–20% of your daily calories. Because saturated and trans fats (see page 16) are not essential and provide no known health benefit, you should eat as little of them as possible. This action will account for most of your calorie saving. Main culprits are likely to be calorie-dense, low-fibre snacks; biscuits, crisps, puddings, ice cream, cakes, and chocolate bars.

## step 4: go for the (slow) burn

Eat more slow-burn foods – oats, beans, lentils, vegetables, fruit – and cut down on fast-releasing carbs that cause rapid rises in blood sugar, white bread, soft drinks and sugary cereals.

Eating carbohydrate with protein or healthy fats balances blood sugar levels better than carbohydrates alone. For example, have potatoes with tuna or a drizzle of olive oil rather than potatoes on their own. This will have a less stimulating effect on insulin, the hormone that drives fat into your fat cells. Slow burn foods (see pages 10–12 on Glycaemic Index) improve appetite regulation and increase feelings of fullness.

## IS HIGH OR LOW INTENSITY BEST FOR FAT BURNING?

High intensity exercise, such as running, burns more fat than low intensity activities such as walking because it burns more calories. It also conditions the heart and lungs better and encourages the body to burn more fat – and less carbohydrate – 24 hours a day. Turning up the intensity will provide the benefits of not only a leaner more defined physique but also improved aerobic fitness and heart health.

Research shows that the best way to improve your fitness and burn fat is with intervals. That is, you alternate very intense periods of work with lower intensity periods, during which you recover. Try one or two minutes of high-intensity alternating with two minutes of recovery. A study at Quebec University found that 90 second bursts at 95% of maximum heart rate) burned three and a half times more body fat than steady-state, moderate-intensity exercise.

# 21 fat-loss tips that work

### 1: eat more frequently

By spreading your meals more evenly through the day, as four to six small meals rather than two or three big ones, you will avoid those blood sugar highs and lows and the resulting insulin surges. Insulin is a powerful anabolic hormone that drives glucose from the bloodstream into muscle cells and, when there's too much glucose around, into your fat cells too. Your aim should be to keep your blood glucose and insulin stable, at levels your body can properly manage. This reduces the chances of fat storage and keeps your metabolism revved throughout the day.

### 2: eat the right foods

Fat makes you fatter than carbohydrates and protein. Because fat is close to the form it needs to be in for storage, metabolising it requires just 3 calories for every 100 you eat. That leaves 97 to be stored in your fat cells. Metabolising carbohydrates requires 10–15 calories, leaving only 85–90 to be stored, whereas protein requires an amazing 20 calories to use it.

So protein and carbohydrate are your best bets if you want to increase your metabolic rate and reduce the amount of excess stored as fat.

### 3: *limit your food choices*

Research at Tufts University in Massachusetts shows that when people are presented with a wider variety of foods they eat considerably more. The message here is to simplify your diet. Next time you are faced with a glorious choice, opt for only two or three types of food rather than a bit of everything. If you must buy high calorie foods, such as biscuits, ice cream or desserts, buy only one variety.

### 4: *practice portion control*

Are you eating more than you need? While you need a certain amount to fuel your training, eating boulder-size portions will result in stored body fat. Try checking your portion sizes against those suggested in the Fitness Food Pyramid (page 2). As a rule of thumb, the carbohydrate (e.g. potato, rice, pasta) and protein (e.g. fish, meat) should be no bigger than the size of your fist.

### 5: *don't skip your favourite foods*

Including your favourite foods in moderation will make your fat loss plan easier to stick to, if not pleasurable. If you know that you can eat a little of your favourite indulgence every day, you'll stop thinking of it as a forbidden food and then won't want to binge on it. So go ahead and include chocolate or ice cream in your nutrition plan but make sure it's only a little.

### 6: *bump up the protein*

When you reduce your calorie intake, the need for protein increases to prevent a loss in muscle tissue and to maintain your metabolic rate. Experts recommend increasing your protein intake by about 0.2g/kg.

Studies have also shown that protein blunts your appetite more than carbohydrate or fat. If you skimp on protein you could find yourself still hungry after you've eaten. Eat a fist-sized portion of protein at each meal.

## 7: *enjoy a good breakfast*

Eating a good breakfast kick-starts your metabolism and allows you the whole day to burn up those calories. Your body is more responsive to insulin in the morning, less so in the evening as your cortisol levels go up. So you're more capable of handling carbohydrates effic-iently in the morning than you are in the evening. Those carbs will be used to fuel your daily activities and work-outs, instead of being stored as body fat if they were eaten in the evening.

If you don't eat breakfast, you're more likely to snack during the morning and over-eat at lunch. Studies have shown that dieters who ate a high fibre breakfast lost more weight than their breakfast-skipping counterparts.

## 8: *don't eat a big evening meal*

Try to eat a smaller meal, comprised mainly of protein and vegetables before going to bed. Try and avoid eating altogether during the two hours before retiring. Eating a lot of calories in the evening when you're inactive increases the chances of storing them as body fat.

## 9: *distinguish between hunger and appetite*

Unfortunately, it is easy to confuse hunger and appetite. Appetite is produced by external stimuli such as the sight or smell of food or simply feeling bored. Real feelings of hunger are produced when your blood sugar begins to fall. The difference is that appetite goes away when you distract yourself with another activity. Next time you feel the urge to eat, distract yourself by going for a walk, taking a bath or doing your nails. If you're still hungry then you know you need to eat.

## 10: *don't be fat phobic*

Don't try to cut fat out completely as this would be unhealthy and hinder your progress. Including foods rich in essential fats – oily fish, avocados, nuts, olives and seeds – in moderation can help you burn body fat more efficiently, improve your aerobic capacity and boost your immunity (see page 14).

## 11: *keep an eye on your drinking*

Alcohol calories count too, and if you happily knock back several drinks in an evening, they can sabotage your fat loss plan. Alcohol calories can't be stored and have to be used as they are consumed – and this means that calories excess to requirements from other foods get stored as fat instead. One small glass of red wine contains 85 calories and a bottle of lager contains 130 calories. If you have a drink, make sure you include it in your daily calorie allowance.

> I used to be typical dieter – always skipping breakfast and lunch to try and save calories but ending up eating a big meal, late in the evening because I was so hungry. Since changing my eating pattern to include a decent breakfast and lunch, I no longer feel so hungry in the evening and I have lost 2 stone of body fat.
>
> SARAH, WEST MIDLANDS

## 12: drink water

Many people confuse thirst with hunger. Both thirst and hunger sensations are generated at the same time to indicate the brain's needs. If you don't recognise the sensation of thirst, you may assume that you are hungry, so you eat instead of drinking water. Next time you're feeling peckish drink a glass of water and wait ten minutes to see if you are still hungry.

## 13: eat fruit instead of drinking juice

Fruit juice and dried fruit contain much higher concentrations of (natural) sugar than the fresh fruit they came from. If you drank two glasses (400 ml) of orange juice a day, you'd be knocking back 180 calories. Switch to water and a whole orange and you'll save 120 calories. Other calorie-saving fruit swaps include substituting a small bunch of grapes (60 calories) for 2 tablespoons (60 g) of raisins (164 calories), choosing an apple (50 calories) instead of a glass of apple juice (90 calories), eating 2 fresh apricots (40 calories) instead of a small pack (87 g) of dried apricots (144 calories).

## 14: beware of 'reduced fat' labels

Eating foods labelled 'reduced-fat' may make you feel virtuous but it can trick your brain into letting you overeat. Many lower fat versions of biscuits, ice cream, cakes and yoghurt contain extra sugar or modified starch in place of the fat, making their calorie count just as high. Unfortunately, the body is not very good at regulating the intake of high calorie food, whether the calories comes from fat or carbohydrate. You may keep eating, thinking you're being good, while actually you're being overloaded with calories. You would be better off eating the occasional biscuit or cake rather than regularly eating the reduced fat versions.

## 15: don't go shopping when you're hungry

If you go shopping when you're hungry you'll be tempted to fill up your trolley with high calorie foods. Make a shopping list before you hit the supermarket. That way you'll avoid unplanned supermarket splurges on unhealthy foods. If you shop with a list you're less likely to make impulsive food choices.

## 16: replace half your carbohydrates with veggies

In the evening, go easy on potatoes, bread and pasta and fill up instead with plenty of vegetables and fresh fruit, as well as lean protein. Try replacing half of your usual portion of pasta (or whatever) with vegetables such as carrots, broccoli, green beans or cauliflower. That way you won't feel like you're eating less.

## 17: match every excuse to a solution

Do you snack on high calorie foods during the day because you're always in a rush? The solution is to prepare meals in advance or, maybe, take a supply of healthy snacks with you if you can't take a long enough break to eat a meal. Do you always snack on high calorie foods in front of the television? Eat an apple instead or, better still, think of an activity to take you away from the television.

## 18: carry healthy snacks

Always carry healthy snacks, such as apples, satsumas or small protein bars, with you so you don't end up at the chocolate vending machine or snack food counter when you're hit by hunger.

## 19: eat soup

Eat a bowl of soup for starters and you'll find that it curbs your appetite. Research at the University of Pennsylvania found that if you have soup as a first course, you end up eating fewer calories. Avoid creamy soups though; stick to vegetable varieties.

## 20 : *watch less TV*

Watching television can make you eat more. Researchers have found that people who watch TV for more than four hours a day consume one third more calories because they have more opportunity to nibble (and less opportunity to exercise).

## 21: *stock up with healthy foods*

Keep a well-stocked supply of healthy foods that you love to make your fat loss programme easy. Decide which new foods you're going to substitute for high fat or sugary ones. This way, you'll keep yourself on track and avoid the temptation of slipping back into old eating habits. Remember, fruit, vegetables, pulses and wholegrain cereals give best filling power for minimum calories. They contain lots of water and fibre, which fill you up, slow down your eating speed and give best meal satisfaction. Choose the ones you like and stock up on those.

# case study

Alison Nicholls' biggest downfall was nibbling all evening in front of the TV. After her evening meal, she would continue eating while watching TV and could easily get through a whole carton of ice-cream or a box of chocolates. Not surprisingly, she found it difficult to manage her weight, despite doing three or four exercise classes a week. After taking a careful look at her diet and lifestyle with me, she decided to face up to the problem. Now she watches less TV but when the TV is on, she eats only low calorie foods such as satsumas or sugar-free jelly. She has lost 8 lb in two months!

### LOW CARBOHYDRATE HIGH PROTEIN DIETS: DO THEY REALLY WORK?

Studies at the University of Cincinnati, Ohio University and Duke University, have shown that people who follow a low carbohydrate, high-protein diet lose weight in the short term. Most of the studies have involved only small numbers of dieters, and there is no evidence that weight loss can be maintained for longer than 6 months. The

American Heart Association has questioned the safety of such diets.

Any diet that restricts calories whether it's high carbohydrate, high protein or high fat, will lead to weight loss. So the fact that people lose substantial amounts of weight on a low carb high protein diet is due almost entirely to its low calorie content. Take out virtually all the starch and sugar from any diet and you automatically restrict the foods that you can eat. You're unlikely to overeat high protein foods, such as meat, fish or eggs.

The theory behind the low carb diet – that too much carbohydrate causes over-production of insulin, which then promotes fat storage – is flawed. Firstly, studies have shown that a high protein meal can result in a larger insulin response than a low GI high carbohydrate meal with a similar calorie content. Secondly, many of the foods that dieters are told to avoid – grains, fruit, carrots – actually have a low glycaemic effect.

A low-carbohydrate diet is totally unsuitable for regular exercisers who need a constant supply of carbohydrate to replenish glycogen stores and fuel their activity. Low carbohydrate diets can have a disastrous effect on performance. They empty your glycogen stores, resulting in reduced endurance, exercise intensity and strength. In this state, your body will also break down protein (muscle) for fuel. Muscle loss causes a knock-on effect of lowering your BMR so your body burns even fewer calories.

For people with the so-called 'thrifty gene' who are predisposed to weight gain and lead sedentary lives, reducing their intake of carbohydrate may be of benefit. By cutting out high-glycaemic refined carbohydrate foods, you not only cut calories but also even out your insulin levels. This simple move will reduce fat storage and promote body fat loss.

The key to fat loss is a diet that is portion controlled and does not contain an excess of calories. It should include all food groups – in particular foods that satisfy your appetite, foods that are high in complex and low glycaemic carbohydrates, contain a modest amount of protein and have a high fibre and water content. Long-term weight control is not about quick fixes; it's about making simple yet lasting changes to the way you eat and incorporating regular activity in your daily schedule.

# sports
# supplements

Do you really need supplements? The claims they make sound so convincing and alluring. They promise to make you healthier, stronger, and leaner. The problem is that there's no systematic regulation of dietary supplements so there's no guarantee that a supplement lives up to its claims. You can't even assume that supplements are safe because they are classified as foods, meaning they don't have to undego safety tests. Worse, some do not even contain the ingredients declared on the label. You need to do your homework before parting with your money. The following guide explains what's in the most popular supplements, whether they work, what the risks are and whether you could benefit from them.

## TIPS FOR EVALUATING A SUPPLEMENT

- don't be taken in by supplements that promise dramatic results. If the manufacturer's claims sound too good to be true, then they probably are.
- be sceptical of adverts that contain lots of technical jargon, unnecessary graphs or big words. If the information isn't clear and factual, leave the supplement well alone.
- be wary of glossy adverts that rely on astonishing before and after photos rather than scientifically sound evidence.
- ask the manufacturer for evidence and studies that support the supplement's claims. If the information isn't available, don't touch that supplement.
- check that any evidence is unbiased. Ideally, studies should have been carried out at a university, not funded solely by the manufacturer, and have been published in a reputable scientific journal.
- don't take a supplement that has been recommended only by word of mouth. Check out exactly what's in it and whether it works before you buy it. Ask an expert if you have any questions.

# antioxidant supplements

## what's in them?

Antioxidant supplements contain various combinations of nutrients and plant extracts including beta-carotene, vitamin C, vitamin E, zinc, magnesium, copper, lycopene (pigment found in tomatoes), selenium, co-enzyme Q10, catechins (found in green tea), methionine (an amino acid), and anthocyanidins (pigments found in purple or red fruit).

## what do they do?

Antioxidants quench potentially harmful free radicals produced in the body. Although your body produces it's own antioxidant enzymes, supplements may boost your natural defences. Studies have linked high intakes of antioxidants from diet and supplements with a reduced a risk of heart disease, certain cancers and cataracts. Supplements may also help slow down the ageing process, promote recovery after intense exercise and reduce post exercise muscle soreness.

## do you need them?

A daily antioxidant supplement should not be a substitute for a healthy diet, but it may give you increased protection from diseases and speed your recovery after a tough workout. Aim to eat at least five portions of fruit and vegetables daily – the more

### WHICH PILLS ARE YOU POPPING?

The most popular supplements are multivitamins, according to a 2002 survey of more than 100 gym regulars. Researchers at the Old Dominion University found that 78% of serious gymgoers take them, followed by protein supplements (67%), creatine (57%), caffeine (48%), androstenedione (15%) and HMB (6%).

I started taking antioxidant supplements during the preparation for my last marathon and now I take them all year round as I feel much better since taking them. They seem to guard against me getting ill, as I haven't had a cold in the last year so. I think it's worth taking them because I feel better!

SUSIE WHALLEY, FOUR TIME LONDON MARATHON RUNNER.

intense the colour, the higher the antioxidant content – as well as healthy oils (such as avocados, oily fish and pure vegetable oils) for their vitamin E content.

## are there any side effects?
No, but keep to the recommended doses on the label.

# caffeine
## what is it?
Caffeine is found in coffee (66–112 mg per cup), tea (average 42 mg per cup), cola (43–65 mg per can), chocolate (average 40 mg per 54 g bar), some energy and sports drinks (up to 100 mg per can) and some energy gels (average 25 mg per serving).

## what does it do?
Taken just before exercise, caffeine encourages the release of fatty acids into your bloodstream. Your muscles then use these fatty acids for fuel, which conserves valuable glycogen. This means that you can work out longer without feeling tired. Caffeine is also a stimulant, boosting concentration and masking fatigue.

## do you need it?
If you have a cup of coffee or caffeinated energy drink about an hour before exercise, it may help you go faster, keep going longer and up the intensity of your workout. Some athletes take caffeine supplements equivalent to several cups of coffee. But in such higher doses, it can cause side effects. If you are sensitive to caffeine, it is best to avoid it altogether.

**DOES CAFFEINE HAVE A DEHYDRATING EFFECT?**
According to studies at University Medical School in Aberdeen, a regular but moderate caffeine intake does not dehydrate the body as was once imagined (see page 31). Only when caffeine is taken in large doses – equivalent to more than 3 cups of coffee – or taken infrequently is it likely to have a noticeable diuretic effect. It appears that people build up a tolerance to caffeine so its diuretic action becomes weakened if you regularly consume it.

## what are the side effects?

Caffeine can cause trembling or shaking, increased fluid losses through urine and restlessness. It also increases your heart rate and breathing rate.

# creatine

## what's in it?

Creatine is a protein made naturally in the body, but can also be found in meat and fish or taken in higher doses as a supplement. It is most commonly taken as a powder mixed with water but liquid forms are also available.

## what does it do?

Creatine combines with phosphorus to form phosphocreatine (PC) in your muscle cells. This is an energy-rich compound that fuels your muscles during high-intensity activity, such as lifting weights or sprinting. Boosting PC levels with supplements enables you to sustain all-out activity longer than usual, and recover faster between bouts or 'sets', resulting in greater strength and improved ability to do repeated sets. Studies have shown that creatine supplements can improve performance in high intensity activities, as well as increase total and lean body weight.

## do you need it?

If you train with weights, sprint or do any sport that includes repeated sprints, jumps or throws (such as rugby, football or sprint cycling), creatine supplements may help increase your strength, muscle mass and performance. But creatine doesn't work for everyone. Some studies have found that creatine made no difference to the performance of athletes. It is unlikely to benefit endurance performance.

**Not everyone benefits from creatine. Some athletes are uncomfortable with the water retention, and others find they get cramps. But I think there is a big placebo effect as my own research found that many people who thought they were taking creatine, but weren't, reported a benefit!**

CLIVE BREWER, SPORTS SCIENTIST, & STRENGTH AND CONDITIONING SPECIALIST

## WHAT IS THE BEST WAY OF TAKING CREATINE?

While most of the manufacturers recommend loading up on creatine to boost levels of creatine in the muscles, others suggest a more moderate dose over a longer period. So which is the best advice? Most of the early research on creatine used a loading dose of 20–25 g daily for 5–7 days, followed by a maintenance dose of 2–5 g daily. This method gives quick results but is more likely to produce side effects such as water retention. Also, the body has to work harder to process the excess creatine as less than 1% of the dose ends up in the muscles. The rest is excreted in some form. More recent research has shown that lower daily doses of 3–7 g (divided into four equal doses) for 30 days gives similar performance results but with less water retention. Canadian researchers found that 7 g daily produces significant increases in workout intensity, power output and muscle size in 21 days. On average, the volunteers gained 2.2 kg of lean body weight.

Researchers recommend taking creatine with carbohydrate because the insulin spike produced by the carbs drives more creatine into the muscles. The exact amount of carbs is debatable but most studies have used between 30 and 90 g. Taking creatine with your normal meals is a cheaper and equally effective option to buying more expensive creatine-carbohydrate products.

## are there any side effects?

The main side effect is weight gain. This is due partly to extra water in the muscle cells and partly to increased muscle tissue. While this is desirable for many gym regulars, it could be disadvantageous if you are an endurance runner or compete in a weight-category sport. Some people find they get water retention, particularly during the loading phase (see 'What is the best way to take

> I took creatine for 3 months pre-season. It definitely improved my explosive power, and my strength and ability to rep out with the weights in the gym.
>
> TOM UPSHER, EX-PROFESSIONAL FOOTBALLER, FULHAM FC

creatine?' p. 71). Other reported side effects include cramps and stomach discomfort, which may be due to dehydration rather than creatine. As larger-than-normal amounts of creatine need to be processed by the kidneys, there is a theoretical long-term risk of kidney damage. While short-term and low-dose creatine supplementation appears to be safe, the effects of long-term and/or high dose creatine supplementation, alone or in combination with other supplements remains unknown.

# fat burners or thermogenics

## *what are they?*

There is an overwhelming array of fat-burning or 'diet' pills supplements that claim to speed your metabolism and shed body fat. Many contain ephedrine or ephedra (from the Chinese herb, ma huang), which is often combined with caffeine and aspirin.

## *what do they do?*

Both ephedrine (which is chemically similar to amphetamines) and caffeine are powerful central nervous system stimulants, which mean they increase heart rate and blood pressure as well as revving the metabolic rate and calorie burn. They appear to boost each other's effects, which is why they are often taken together. Aspirin is also sometimes added as it may prolong the stimulant activity of the other two. No one knows the precise action but it is thought that when you take them, you temporarily supercharge the nervous system, causing an increase in heat production (or thermogenesis) and release of stored fat. Studies have shown that these supplements do indeed enhance fat loss when taken with a low calorie diet. The problem is that they can also cause harmful side effects.

## *do you need them?*

The International Olympic Committee (IOC) bans ephedrine and caffeine – though caffeine must present in high concentrations in the urine. In October 2002 the American Medical Association called for a ban on sales of ephedrine in light of recent cases of heart attacks, strokes and deaths associated with its use. My advice is to keep clear of any fat burner containing ephedrine (or ma huang) because of the significant health risks. Exercise and good nutrition are the best methods for burning fat.

### are there any side effects?

The doses necessary to cause a fat-burning effect are quite high and are associated with a number of risky side effects including an increased and irregular heartbeat, a rise in blood pressure, irritability, dizziness, and other symptoms of nervousness (or being 'hyper'). They are also addictive. More severe consequences such as heart attack, stroke and death have been reported in the medical press. Taking the ephedrine-caffeine-aspirin stack increases the chance of side effects.

# fat burners (ephedrine-free)

### what are they?

Other fat-burning pills and capsules claim to mimic the effect of ephedrine - to boost the metabolism and enhance fat loss – but without the harmful side effects. The most popular ingredients include citrus aurantium (synephrine or bitter orange extract), green tea extract and forskolin extract (a herb).

### what do they do?

Citrus aurantium is related to ephedrine but has a much weaker stimulating effect on the nervous system. Green tea extract contains polyphenols (antioxidants) that may enhance fat burning and increase the metabolic rate. Initial research suggests that it may cause a greater proportion of fat versus carbohydrate to be burned for energy. Forskolin extract also appears to boost metabolism and stimulate the release of stored fat.

### do you need them?

The research on ephedrine-free fat burners is only preliminary and any fat burning boost they provide is relatively small (less than 100 calories a day). The doses used in some brands may be too small to provide a measurable effect. Again, sensible eating and exercise are likely to produce better results in the long term. Drinking green tea will boost your antioxidant intake but probably won't enhance fat burning.

### are there any side effects?

While the herbal alternatives to ephedrine are generally safer, you may get side effects with high doses. Citrus aurantium can increase blood pressure as much as if not more than ephedrine. High doses of forskolin may cause heart disturbances.

# glutamine

### what is it?

Glutamine supplements come as powders (which you mix with water or add to a protein shake) and capsules. It is a non-essential amino acid found abundantly in the muscle cells and blood.

### what does it do?

It is needed for cell growth as well as serving as a fuel for the immune system. During periods of heavy training or stress, blood levels of glutamine fall, weakening your immune system and putting you at risk of infection. Muscle levels of glutamine also fall, which results in a loss of muscle tissue despite continued training.

### do you need it?

The evidence for gutamine is divided. Some studies have shown that it can help you recover faster, reduce muscle soreness and cut your risk of catching colds and other infections after heavy training. Others have failed to show any benefits.

### are there any side effects?

No side effects have been found so far.

# HMB
## (Beta-hydroxy beta-methyl butyrate)

### what is it?

HMB is the by-product of the body's normal breakdown of leucine (an essential amino acid). It can be taken as pills or capsules.

### what does it do?
It is involved with the repair and growth of muscle cells. Some studies have suggested that HMB may reduce muscle breakdown, promote faster muscle repair. Other studies suggest that HMB can add up to one kilo of muscle per month as well as boosting strength gains and increase muscle mass in novice gym goers. It may also have a small fat-loss effect. But these benefits have not been found in all athletics. One Australian/Singaporean study found that 6 weeks of HMB supplementation had no effect all at on the strength and muscle mass gains in trained athletes.

### do you need it?
If you're new to lifting weights, HMB may help boost your strength and build muscle. But it is unlikely to be useful to move experienced gym-goers.

### are there any side effects?
No side effects have yet been found.

# multivitamin and mineral supplements

### what's in them?
Multivitamins and mineral pills contain a mixture of micronutrients. In food-state supplements the micronutrients are combined with a yeast base to mimic the form the nutrients occur in food, and increase the amount absorbed by the body.

### what do they do?
Supplements will make up any shortfall in your diet and boost your nutritional status. If your diet is poor, supplements will help improve your health, resistance to infection, and post-workout recovery. But there's no evidence that high doses enhance exercise performance.

### do you need them?
Most people would probably benefit from taking a supplement, but popping a pill can't erase the health effects of a poor diet and sedentary

lifestyle. Go for real food first and take regular exercise. If you workout intensely several times a week, your requirements for many vitamins and minerals will be greater than the RDAs (see box below) so supplements may help you meet your needs better. A deficiency of any vitamin and mineral will impair your health as well as your performance.

I take creatine to improve my recovery after intensive bouts of exercise, and vitamin C, which helps me fight off colds and infections. Apart from that, I just eat healthily with plenty of carbohydrates, fresh fruit and vegetables.

KAJ JACKSON, 2002 COMMONWEALTH
MEN'S GYMNASTICS CHAMPION

## *are there any side effects?*

Side effects are unlikely if you stick to the recommended doses on the label. Check the quantities do not exceed the upper safe levels shown in the table on page 78.

### WHAT ARE RDAS?

The Recommended Daily Amounts (RDAs) listed on food and supplement labels are rough estimates of nutrient requirements, set by the EU and designed to cover the needs of the majority of a population. The amounts are designed to prevent deficiency symptoms, allow for a little storage, as well as covering differences in needs from one person to the next. They are not targets; rather they are guides to help you check that you are probably getting enough nutrients. Regular exercisers may, however, require more than the RDAs so may benefit from a multivitamin and mineral supplement. If you think that you may be deficient in a particular nutrient, consult a G.P., qualified nutritionist or dietitian.

## ARE YOU DEFICIENT IN VITAMINS AND MINERALS?

About 12 million people in the UK take vitamin and mineral supplements to prevent or alleviate illnesses. A study published in the Journal of the American Medical Association concluded that most people do not get enough vitamins in their diet to protect themselves properly from diseases such as cancer and heart disease. Researchers at the Harvard Medical School say that most people would benefit from taking a multivitamin, especially if:

1 You are dieting or eating fewer than 1500 calories daily. Restricting your food intake makes it more likely that you are missing out on certain nutrients.

2 You rely mainly on processed or fast foods. These foods are not only high in saturated fat, sugar and salt but also depleted in vitamins.

3 You regularly skip meals. This means that you are more likely to eat high calorie snacks that are low in vitamins and minerals.

4 You don't eat the recommended five portions of fruit and vegetable daily. These foods are rich in vitamins, minerals and antioxidants.

5 You have a food intolerance or allergy. It may be harder to get some of the nutrients you need.

6 You are a vegan. It's more difficult (though not impossible) to get enough vitamin $B_{12}$, calcium and iron from a plant-based diet.

7 You are pregnant. Take a supplement containing 0.4 mg of folic acid and follow the advice of your midwife or doctor.

## 6.1 the essential guide to vitamins and minerals

| vitamin/mineral | how much?* | why is it needed? | why supplements may benefit you | best food sources | side effects |
|---|---|---|---|---|---|
| **Vitamin A** | 700 mg (men 600 mg (women) no SUL FSA advises max 1500 g | Helps vision in dim light; promotes healthy skin | Maintain normal vision and healthy skin | Liver, cheese, oily fish, eggs, butter, margarine | Liver and bone damage; can harm the unborn baby in pregnant women (avoid during pregnancy). |
| **Carotenoids** | No official RNI 15 mg beta-carotene suggested SUL = 7 mg | Vision in dim light; healthy skin; converts into vitamin A | As antioxidants, may protect against certain cancers, and reduce muscle soreness. Exercise increases need for antioxidants | Intensely coloured fruit and vegetables e.g. apricots, peppers, tomatoes, mangos, broccoli | Excessive doses of beta-carotene can cause harmless orange tinge to skin. Reversible |
| **Thiamin** | 0.4 mg/1000 kcal no SUL 100 mg recommended by FSA | Converts carbohydrates to energy | To process the extra carbohydrate eaten | Wholemeal bread and cereals; pulses; meat | Excess is excreted so toxicity is rare |

| | | | | | |
|---|---|---|---|---|---|
| **Riboflavin** | 1.3 mg (men) 1.1 mg (women) no SUL 40 mg recommended by FSA | Converts carbohydrates to energy | To process the extra carbohydrate eaten | Milk and dairy products; meat; eggs | Excess is excreted (producing yellow urine!) so toxicity is rare |
| **Niacin** | 6.6 mg/1000 kcal SUL = 17 mg from supplements | Converts carbohydrates to energy | To process the extra carbohydrate eaten | Meat and offal; nuts; milk and dairy products; eggs; wholegrain cereals | Excess is excreted. High doses may cause hot flushes |
| **Vitamin C** | 40 mg SUL = 1000 mg | Healthy connective tissue, bones, teeth, blood vessels, gums and teeth; promotes immune function; helps iron absorption | Exercise increases need for antioxidants; may help reduce free radical damage, protect cell membranes and reduce post-exercise muscle soreness | Fruit and vegetables (e.g. raspberries, blackcurrants, kiwi, oranges, peppers, broccoli, cabbage, tomatoes) | Excess is excreted. Doses over 2 g may lead to diarrhoea and excess urine formation. High doses (>2 g) may cause vitamin C to behave as a pro-oxidant (enhance free radical damage) |

continued ...

## 6.1 the essential guide to vitamins and minerals – continued

| vitamin/mineral | how much?* | why is it needed? | why supplements- may benefit you | best food sources | side effects |
|---|---|---|---|---|---|
| **Vitamin E** | No RNI in UK. 10 mg in EU SUL = 540 mg | Antioxidant which helps protect against heart disease; promote normal cell growth and development | Exercise increases need for antioxidants; may help reduce free radical damage, protect cell membranes and reduce post-exercise muscle soreness | Vegetable oils; margarine, oily fish; nuts; seeds; egg yolk; avocado | Toxicity is rare |
| **Calcium** | 1000 mg (men) 700 mg (women) SUL = 1500 mg | Builds bone and teeth; blood clotting; nerve and muscle function | Low oestrogen in female athletes with amenorrhoea increases bone loss and need for calcium | Milk and dairy products; sardines; dark green leafy vegetables; pulses; nuts and seeds | High intakes may interfere with absorption of other minerals. Take with magnesium and vitamin D |
| **Iron** | 8.7 mg (men) 14.8 mg (women) SUL = 17 mg | Formation of red blood cells, oxygen transport; prevents anaemia | Female athletes may need more to compensate for menstrual losses | Meat and offal; wholegrain cereals; fortified breakfast cereals; pulses; | Constipation, stomach dis- comfort. Avoid unnecessary |

| | | | greenleafy vegetables | supplementation – may increase free radical damage |
|---|---|---|---|---|
| **Zinc** | 9.5 mg (men) 7.0 mg (women) SUL = 25 mg | Healthy immune system; wound healing; skin; cell growth | Exercise increases need for antioxidants; may help immune function | Eggs; wholegrain cereals; meat; milk and dairy products | Interferes with absorption of iron and copper |
| **Magnesium** | 300 mg (men) 270 mg (women) SUL = 400 mg | Healthy bones muscle and nerve function; cell formation | May improve recovery after strength training; increase aerobic capacity | Cereals; fruit; vegetables; milk | May cause diarrhoea |
| **Potassium** | 3500 mg SUL = 3700 mg from supplements | Fluid balance; muscle and nerve function | May help prevent cramp | Fruit; vegetables; cereals | Excess is excreted |
| **Selenium** | 75 ug (men) 60 ug (women) SUL = 350 ug | Antioxidant which helps protect against heart disease and cancer | Exercise increases free radical production | Cereals; vegetables; dairy products; meat; eggs | Nausea, vomiting, hair loss |

**Notes:**
mg= milligrams (1000 mg = 1 gram)
ug = micrograms (1000 ug = 1 mg)
*The amount needed is given as the Reference Nutrient Intake (RNI, Dept of Health, 1991). This is the amount of a nutrient that should cover the needs of 97% of the population. Athletes in hard training may need more.

SUL = Safe Upper Limit recommended by the Export Group on Vitamins and Minerals, an independent advisory committee to the Food Standards Agency (FSA).

# prohormones/ steroid precursors

## what are they?

Prohormone supplements, including DHEA, androstenedione (or andro for short) and norandrostenedione are marketed to bodybuilders and other athletes looking to pack on strength and size.

## what do they do?

Manufacturers claim the supplements will increase testosterone levels in the body and produce similar muscle-building effects to anabolic steroids but without the side effects. However, researchers at Iowa State University found that andro and DHEA supplements do not elevate testosterone, nor do they live up to their claims of increasing strength and muscle mass. Higher doses than those recommended on supplement labels may raise testosterone but there's no evidence that this results in greater muscle mass or strength.

## do you need them?

It is unlikely that prohormones work and they may produce

### SOON TO BE BANNED?

Currently, prohormones are legal to buy but proposed legislation (in 2002) by lawmakers in US wants to have them listed as banned substances. The International Olympic Committee has warned athletes to avoid supple-ments containing these prohor-mones or risk testing positive for steroid use.

unwanted side effects. What's more, their contents can't always be guaranteed. In tests carried out by the International Olympic Committee, 15% of the supplements contained substances that would lead to a failed drugs test, including nandrolone, despite them not being listed on the label.

### are there any side effects?

Studies have found that most prohormones increase oestrogen (which can lead to breast development) and decrease HDL (good cholesterol) levels. Some supplements include anti-oestrogen substances such as chrysin but there is yet no evidence that they work either.

# protein powders

### what's in them?

Protein powders contain mostly whey protein, which is derived from milk.

### what do they do?

They give you extra protein in a form that claims to be better absorbed than food protein. Whey protein may also boost your immune system and protect against muscle breakdown during intense training.

### do you need them?

If you train with weights or include lots of power and strength work in your fitness programme, you will have higher protein needs than normal. Most experts recommend an intake between 1.4 and 1.8 g per kg body weight per day (see page 99). Whether you prefer to get your protein entirely from real food or from supplements too is up to you.

### are there any side effects?

Side effects are unlikely.

# sports foods
# and drinks

What are the best foods for eating on the run? Are sports products better for you than ordinary foods? Do you need a sports drink?
Here's the lowdown on popular sports foods and healthy snacks.

**BREAKFAST BARS**
*Why they're good*: They make a healthy convenient snack that – provided you choose the right brands – is lower in fat and sugar, higher in fibre and vitamins than confectionery bars. Like nutrition and energy bars, they are convenient to carry around, and they work out cheaper. But some brands are deceptively high in fats (including harmful hydrogenated fats) and sugar and low in fibre. Most provide between 130 and 180 calories per bar.

*When they're good*: Whenever you need a quick boost of energy, during long cycle rides or straight after a workout.

## energy bars
*what are they?*
Energy bars are made from carbohydrate- rich ingredients; maltodextrin, corn syrup, sugars, dried fruit or cereal. Most provide around 200 calories and 50 g of carbohydrate per bar with very little protein or fat.

*what do they do?*
Energy bars provide a quick energy-fix and solid carbs are as good as liquid carbs when it comes to fuelling before, during and after exercise. University of Sydney researchers found that low glycaemic solid carbs eaten before training improved endurance because they provide a sustained release of energy. Another Australian study with cyclists compared an energy bar (plus water) with a sports drink during exercise.

Both boosted blood sugar levels and endurance. Researchers at Cornell University, New York, found that solid and liquid carbs were again equally effective in promoting glycogen re-fuelling after intense and prolonged exercise.

### do you need them?

The main benefit of energy bars is their convenience. They are easy to carry and provide variety during or after exercise. Make sure that you have your bar with enough water (at least 250 ml) to replace fluids lost in sweat as well as to digest the bar. Check the label as some brands are loaded with pure sugar (glucose, corn syrup, fructose, etc), which may cause a surge in insulin and send your blood sugar level plummeting back down. The box on the next page will help you choose the right bar.

### are there any side effects?

There are no side effects except, possibly, the risk of fat gain, if you consume too many calories.

---

**HOW TO CHOOSE THE RIGHT ENERGY BAR**

- choose a bar that contains between 30–60 g of carbs.
- avoid those that list corn syrup, sugar, glucose or sweeteners in the first few ingredients.
- check that the bar contains no more than 4 g of fat per 200 calories.
- try different brands until you find one with the right taste and texture for you.
- For a cheaper alternative, you may want to try cereal bars and breakfast bars (see boxes).

---

# energy gels

### what are they?

Energy gels come in small squeezy sachets and have a 'gloopy' jelly-like texture. They consist almost entirely of simple sugars (such as fructose and glucose) and maltodextrin (a carbohydrate consisting of 4–20 glucose units). They may also contain sodium, potassium and caffeine. Most contain between 18–25 g of carbohydrate per sachet.

### what do they do?

Gels provide a concentrated source of calories and carbohydrate, designed to be consumed during endurance exercise. Studies show that consuming 30–60 g of carbohydrate per hour during prolonged exercise delays fatigue and improves endurance. This translates into 1–2 sachets per hour. One study showed that gels have a similar effect on blood sugar levels and performance as sports drinks.

### do you need them?

Gels provide a convenient way of consuming carbohydrate during intense endurance exercise lasting longer than an hour. But you need to drink around 200 ml of water with each gel sachet. Try them as an alternative to sports drinks and bars. On the downside, some people dislike their texture, sweetness and intensity of flavour – it's really down to personal preference – and they don't do away with the need for carrying a water bottle with you.

### are there any side effects?

There are no risky side effects. Remember, though, that energy gels don't hydrate you so you must drink plenty of water with them.

---

### CEREAL BARS

*Why they're good*: If you choose the right bar you have a handy snack that's high in carbohydrate, lower in fat and higher in fibre than confectionery bars. Most bars provide between 120 and 180 calories. However, some brands are loaded with hydrogenated fat, sugar and glucose syrup – not what you need to fuel your body. Choose bars that contain less than 5 g of fat per bar (not hydrogenated or palm kernel oil) and include naturally sweet ingredients, such as dried fruit, rather than large amounts of sugar.

*When they're good*: When you need to refuel in a hurry.

# meal replacement shakes

*what's in them?*

Shakes contain a mixture of concentrated milk proteins (usually whey protein and casein), carbohydrate (maltodextrin and/ or sugars), vitamins and minerals. Some brands also contain small amounts of oil and other substances that claim to boost health and performance.

*what do they do?*

They provide a well-balanced and convenient alternative to solid food.

*do you need them?*

They will not necessarily improve your performance but can be a helpful addition (rather than replacement) to your diet if you struggle to eat enough real food, you need eat on the move or you need the extra protein they provide.

**If you have trouble fitting regular meals into a busy schedule, you can use meal replacement drinks or bars. But try to select products that are nutritious and well balanced and avoid those containing large amounts of refined sugar or fat.**

KESH PATEL, EXERCISE SPECIALIST

*are there any side effects?*

Side effects are unlikely.

## DRIED FRUIT

*Why they're good*: Raisins, sultanas, dried apricots, dried mangos etc. are concentrated sources of carbohydrates, which makes them useful when you need a quick energy boost. As they are dried, they also provide concentrated fibre, potassium, phytonutrients, vitamins and minerals. Apricots are rich in beta-carotene; prunes and raisins are one of the best antioxidant foods, according to a study at Tufts University (see page 20).

*When they're good*: They make handy snacks for eating on the go. Have a handful with a drink of water after exercise (with water) to speed up glycogen refuelling. Try them also on long cycle rides, but don't overdo it as the fibre content may upset your stomach.

# nutrition (sports) bars

*what are they?*

Nutrition – or sports, protein or meal replacement – bars differ from energy bars because, in addition to a carbohydrate source (such as maltodextrin, sugars, dried fruit) they also provide a protein source (such as whey protein, milk protein or soy protein) vitamins, herbs, glutamine and amino acids. They provide around 200–350 calories, 20–50 g of carbohydrate and 15–30 g of protein.

*what do they do?*

They provide calories, carbohydrate, protein and vitamins in a convenient and portable form. Regard nutrition bars as an alternative to real food, providing a similar balance of nutrients to a nutritious snack or mini-meal.

*do you need them?*

Nutrition bars are good for eating on the move. They are convenient and easy to carry with you, and a better choice than popular snack or confectionery bars. Like energy bars, they provide variety before or after exercise.

*are there any side effects?*

There are no side effects.

## HOW TO CHOOSE THE RIGHT NUTRITION BAR

- go for a bar that contains between two to three times as much carbohydrate as protein.
- choose a bar that contains whey, milk protein, soy or casein protein, rather than hydrolysed gelatine.
- steer clear of bars that list corn syrup, sugar syrup, glucose or sweeteners as their main ingredients.
- check the bar contains no more than 4 g of fat per 200 calories and doesn't include palm kernel oil or hydrogenated fat.
- check that it contains at least one sixth of the RDA for vitamins and minerals.

## nutty flapjacks

*Here's one of my favourite nutrition bar recipes. It provides slow-release carbohydrates, protein and essential fats, ideal for carrying in your kit bag and re-fuelling between tough workouts. You can add extra raisins, dried apricots or cherries if you wish.*

**makes 12 flapjacks**

150 g (5 oz) butter or margarine
60 g (2 oz) light brown sugar
5 tbsp golden syrup
200 g (7 oz) porridge oats
30 g (1 oz) desiccated coconut
125 g (4 oz) Brazil nuts, roughly
chopped
60 g (2 oz) almonds, roughly chopped

- Pre heat the oven to 180°C/350°F/Gas mark 4. Lightly oil a 23 cm (9 inch) square baking tin.
- Put the butter or margarine, sugar and syrup in a heavy-based saucepan and heat together, stirring occasionally, until the butter has melted. Remove from the heat.
- Mix in the oats, coconut, Brazils and almonds until thoroughly combined.
- Transfer the mixture into the prepared tin, level the surface and bake in the oven for 20–25 minutes until golden brown around the edges but still soft in the middle. Leave in the tin to cool. While still warm, score into 12 bars with a sharp knife.

# sports drinks
*what are they?*

Sports drinks are designed to provide fluid, carbohydrate (in the form of sucrose, glucose, fructose and maltodextrin) and electrolytes (sodium and potassium) more rapidly than plain water. They fall into 2 categories; (a) fluid replacement drinks containing around 4–8 g carbohydrate per 100 ml. (b) energy drinks containing 12–20 g carbohydrate per 100 ml.

## FRUIT YOGHURT

*Why it's good*: Yoghurt contains a near-perfect combination of carbohydrate (lactose, or milk sugar, and sucrose) and protein suitable for post-workout recovery. It's also low in fat and a great source of calcium and B vitamins. 'Bio' yoghurts contain beneficial bacteria that can boost your immune system.

*When it's good*: Any time. It's particularly good for after intense workouts as the protein-carbohydrate combination encourages faster glycogen recovery than carbohydrate alone.

## what do they do?

They serve the dual purpose of providing fluid as well as fuel for active muscles. The sugars and maltodextrin in isotonic drinks speed up the absorption of water from your gut into your bloodstream. The sodium in sports drinks is designed to stimulate drinking (salt makes you thirsty) and help your body retain the fluid better. Research from the University of Texas found that drinking water during one hour of cycling improved performance by 6% compared with no water, but drinking a sugar-containing drink resulted in a 12% improvement on performance.

## do you need them?

If you are working out continually for longer than 60 minutes, a sports drink – instead of water – may help you keep going longer or work out harder. Drink between 500ml and one litre per hour of your workout (see page 40). If you haven't eaten for more than four hours, try a pre-workout sports drink. If you work out for between 1 and 2 hours, choose drinks containing less than 8 g sugar per 100 ml; for intense workouts lasting longer than two hours, try an energy drink based on maltodextrin. For a less expensive

**Don't think you have to buy expensive shop-bought sports drinks. Get creative in the kitchen and keep trying out new recipes until you hit on the best sports drink for you.**

RACHEL ANN HILL, REGISTERED NUTRITIONIST

alternative, try mixing fruit juice with equal quantities of water. This produces an isotonic drink with around 6 g sugar per 100 ml. Add a pinch (one quarter of a teaspoon) of ordinary salt if you sweat heavily.

## are there any side effects?

Side effects are unlikely provided you stick to the recommended dilution on the label. Avoid caffeine- and ephedrine-containing drinks if you are sensitive to the side effects (see page 77 and 80).

### BANANAS

*Why they're good*: Bananas are filling, healthy and full of nutrients. An average banana provides around 90 calories and 15 g of carbohydrate, is high in fibre, potassium and vitamin $B_6$. They are the ultimate convenience food, easy to carry around with you and easy to eat during cycling or between heats.

*When they're good*: Eat them 30–60 minutes before exercise, during workouts lasting more than an hour or right after training. Eat them on their own or whiz up with some milk, yoghurt and maybe some strawberries for a delicious recovery smoothie.

### SMOOTHIES

*Why they're good*: Smoothies made with fresh fruit are a great way of meeting your five-a-day target for fruit and vegetables. Avoid the ready-bought vers-ions that contain added sugar and artificial additives. Best option is to make your own by whizzing fresh fruit (such as berries, bananas and pears) with a little fruit juice or yoghurt. Smoothies are packed with beta-carotene, vitamin C, phyt-onutrients and, because you whizz up the whole fruit, fibre too.

*When they're good*: For breakfast, as a 'snack', or as a refreshing post-workout drink.

# banana and almond smoothie

*This drink provides an almost perfect balance of protein, carbohydrate and healthy fats, and makes an ideal liquid meal in between intense workouts. Almonds are rich in vitamin E, calcium and protein, the milk provides extra protein and calcium and the bananas supply magnesium, potassium and vitamin $B_6$.*

**makes 2 drinks**   8–10 ice cubes
400 ml (14 fl oz) low fat milk
2 ripe bananas, roughly chopped
60 g (2 oz) ground almonds
1 tbsp (15 ml) clear honey

- Place the ice cubes in the goblet of a smoothie maker, blender or food processor and process until slushy.
- Add the milk, bananas, almonds and honey and process until thick and frothy. Chill in the fridge or drink immediately.

## PORRIDGE

*Why it's good*: Porridge is a low glycaemic food, which produces a slow sustained blood sugar rise. It's therefore good for keeping your energy levels up, and boosting glycogen stores with minimal risk of turning into body fat. As a bonus, porridge is filling and satisfying so stops you feeling hungry.

*When it's good*: It's the perfect food for breakfast or for eating 2–4 hours before a workout.

# eating for the gym

Whether you lift weights to get stronger, build muscle or improve your muscle definition, you need a smart eating plan to complement your gym programme. Eating right will produce better results more quickly.

Perhaps you are naturally very lean and struggle endlessly to add more weight ('hard gainer'). Or maybe you find it difficult to build muscle without gaining fat and need to achieve better muscle definition. Either way, the answer lies in devising an eating plan that allows you to put on muscle without unwanted fat.

## training for muscle building

To build muscle you need to combine proper weight training with smart eating. The idea is to stress the muscles just hard enough during your workout to break down muscle proteins and cause very small (micro) tears in the fibres. During the rest period between workouts, new protein is added to the fibres, making the muscle stronger and denser. Not only does the resulting muscle burn more calories, but the muscle-building process also requires extra energy, which your body can take from stored body fat. So you burn more calories while building muscle. Here are some training tips:

**1** Aim for 8–12 sets on large muscle groups (i.e. legs, chest, back, shoulders) and 3–6 sets on small muscle groups (i.e. biceps, triceps).

**2** Perform between 6–12 repetitions with a weight that allows you to complete the set safely; the last repetition should feel extremely hard and you should be unable to complete another one in proper form.

**3** The rest period between sets should be 60–90 seconds and 1–2 minutes between different exercises to allow time for the muscle fibres to partially recover.

**4** You'll get the fastest strength and muscle gains by selecting compound movements (such as bench press, leg press, shoulder press) that stimulate the largest muscle groups. Bodybuilders use at least 2 different exercises per muscle group and use a split system (see over) to allow them to train more intensely.

**5** Training with proper form not only avoids injury but also produces better results. Use a weight that allows you to use a full range of movement, taking the muscle from its fully extended to its fully contracted position. Slow down to about 2 seconds to lift a weight and 3 seconds to lower it.

If you have been lifting weights for a while but haven't been progressing, here are some tips to take your training to the next level:

## split your workouts
Try dividing the exercises you perform for different muscle groups over two or three days. For example, working chest and back on day 1, legs and calves on day 2, and shoulders, biceps and triceps on day 3. Even if you already split your workout, try new pairings to break up your old routine. You'll be surprised at how much you can lift when you perform exercises in a different order.

## kick up the intensity
Push up the intensity by either adding extra repetitions (be it forced reps in which a partner helps you push past your sticking point to complete extra reps, or partial reps in which you do the last few reps through a shorter range of motion), increasing the weights (and doing slightly fewer repetitions) or taking less rest between sets.

## change your exercises
Learn new movements and use them in your workout. Every movement emphasises different muscle fibres so performing a greater variety of exercises stimulates more fibres.

## change your workout
Your muscles quickly adapt to the same old routine – not to mention you getting bored with it – and so they stop growing. To progress, you need to constantly challenge your muscles by changing your workout every

four weeks or so. Try changing the order in which you perform your exercises, occasionally working from smallest to largest muscles ('pre-exhaustion'), performing supersets (performing two exercises in a row with minimal rest), changing the amount of weight and number of reps, or using other advanced techniques such as descending sets (performing reps to failure followed immediately by further reps using a lighter weight).

## *find a training partner*

Training with a partner or personal trainer motivates you to work harder and can make training more fun. You can also do some advanced training techniques, such as forced reps and negative reps (where a heavier weight is used, your partner assists the lifting phase and you lower the weight very slowly, resisting the movement) extending a set past the point where you'd normally stop.

# training for muscle definition

To improve muscle definition, you need to reduce your body fat. It's a myth that doing high repetitions of light weights produces definition – it improves muscle endurance but isn't the best way of burning fat. See pages 55–57 (Chapter 5) for more information on fat burning exercise.

## get your calories right

Your number one concern should be achieving the right calorie intake. Hard gainers will need to step up calories while those looking to achieve muscle definition may need to cut down the calories. So how many calories do you need?

### *for weight gain:*

For weight gain, most scientists recommend upping calories by about 20%. In practice, men will probably need to add 500–1000 calories a day to their usual daily intake; women should add 250–500 extra calories daily. See the box below: 'How many calories do I need?'

How many calories is enough? Check your weight and body fat percentage (see 'Body fat' page 52). If you put on between 0.25 and 0.5 kg (½–1 lb) a week, you're probably eating enough calories. If your weight remains the same, you aren't eating enough to support your training and growth.

## for muscle definition

Adding extra aerobic work to your weights workout may be all that you need to improve your muscle definition. Three 20–40 minute sessions a week should do the trick (see on pages 55–57). But if you are carrying more than 15% (for a man) or 25% (for a women) body fat you may need to cut back your calories too. Try reducing your daily calories by around 15% of your usual intake – that's about 400 calories for men and 300 for women. Think in terms of cutting out one chocolate bar (300 calories) or a couple of packets of crisps (296–370 calories) or 4 chocolate biscuits (336 calories).

Be careful, though, of cutting calories too low. Eating too few calories puts your body into famine mode, where your body thinks that it's starving and starts to hoard fat. Your basal (see page 60) metabolic rate

### HOW MANY CALORIES DO I NEED?

Record your food intake for seven days. Be as accurate as possible, noting the exact weights of all foods and drinks consumed. Use food tables, the Internet or food labels to work out your daily calorie intake. Add up all seven days then divide by seven to get a daily average. Add 20% to that number (multiply by 1.2). This is your new calorie intake to start adding muscle.

### CHECK YOUR BODY FAT

Measuring your body fat percentage using skinfold callipers or bioelectrical imped-ance will tell you how much of you is muscle and how much if you is fat . In gaining weight, expect some of that to be fat. If you put on 3 kg of muscle and 1 kg of fat, you're making great progress. If you gained 2 kg of muscle and 2 kg of fat over the same period, you know your overall calorie and carbohydrate intake is too high, pushing up body fat levels.

slows down and your body turns to muscle (protein) for fuel. Low-carbohydrate dieting will not improve your body composition; instead it will leave you feeling drained, lethargic and, paradoxically, with less muscle mass (see pages 64–65).

## protein is key

Protein is the next most important part of your weight training diet. The building blocks of protein – amino acids – are used for repairing the muscle fibres that you have damaged during your workout. Without sufficient protein, you may as well kiss your muscle growth goodbye.

If you're working out intensely in the gym at least 3 times a week you will need between 1.4 and 1.8 g of protein per kg of bodyweight daily. If you weigh 70 kg, that equals 98–126 g daily. Some bodybuilders eat 2 g or more per kg bodyweight but research at McMaster University, Ontario shows that 1.4–1.8 g is more than enough to cover the protein needs of training. Higher intakes do not result in further increases in strength or muscle size and may even be stored as fat.

In my efforts to build muscle and shed body fat, I used to skip breakfast and go straight down the gym to workout. Unfortunately, this had no effect on my body fat levels; instead I struggled to get through my workout. Now I have a highly nutritious homemade shake (made from protein powder, oats and fruit juice) a couple of hours before training in the morning. I can train longer and harder. Best of all, I've shed some fat, built some muscle and feel terrific!

PAUL NICHOLLS, SURREY

Spread your protein evenly over 5 or 6 meals each day. This will maximise absorption and minimise fat gain. For example, a 70 kg weight trainer who needs 126 g a day could have 25 g in each of five meals or 21 g in each of six meals.

Most gym goers can get enough protein from 2–4 daily portions of chicken, fish, dairy products, eggs and pulses (see page 7). Even vegetarians can meet their protein needs by eating a variety of plant proteins – tofu, quorn, beans, lentils, nuts – each day. Table 8.1 over the page gives the protein content of various foods.

## 8.1 some good protein sources

| food | protein (g) |
|---|---|
| **meat and fish:** | |
| 1 lean fillet steak (105 g) | 31 |
| 1 chicken breast fillet (125 g) | 30 |
| 2 slices turkey breast (40 g) | 10 |
| 1 salmon fillet (150 g) | 30 |
| tuna, canned in brine | 24 |
| **dairy products:** | |
| 1 slice (40 g) cheddar cheese | 10 |
| 2 tablespoons (112g) cottage cheese | 15 |
| 1 glass (200 ml) skimmed milk | 7 |
| 1 glass (200 ml) soya milk | 7 |
| 1 carton yoghurt (150 g) | 6 |
| 1 egg (size 2) | 8 |
| **nuts and seeds:** | |
| 1 handful (50 g) peanuts | 12 |
| 1 tbsp (20 g) peanut butter | 5 |
| **pulses:** | |
| 1 small tin (205 g) baked beans | 10 |
| 3 tbsps (120g) cooked lentils | 9 |
| 3 tbsps (120g) cooked red kidney beans | 10 |
| **soya and quorn products:** | |
| 1 tofu burger (60 g) | 5 |
| 1 quorn burger (50 g) | 6 |
| **grains and cereals:** | |
| 2 slices wholemeal bread | 6 |
| 1 serving (230 g) cooked pasta | 7 |
| **protein supplements:** | |
| 1 scoop (32 g) protein powder | 22* |
| 1 serving (76 g) meal replacement shake | 42* |
| 1 nutrition (sports) bar (50 g) | 15* |

*values may vary depending on brand

## DO I NEED PROTEIN SUPPLEMENTS?

Taking protein supplements won't necessarily give you bigger gains nor will they compensate for a poorly planned diet. The 2002 report from the US National Sciences Institute of Medicine states that there is no evidence to show that healthy people, including bodybuilders, need supplements. However, they can help make up a protein shortfall in the diets of athletes with particularly high nutritional needs – due to a high body weight or heavy training – or regular exercisers who eat a vegetarian or vegan diet. Most meal replacement products and protein supplements are well balanced, convenient, and the whey proteins in them may help boost your immunity during intense training periods. (see pages 83 and 88).

## sample meal plan for a gym goer

| | |
|---|---|
| **breakfast:** | 1 cup (85 g) porridge oats<br>2 cups (400 ml) skimmed milk<br>1 handful (40 g) of raisins |
| **morning snack:** | 2 cartons (2 x 150 g) yoghurt |
| **lunch:** | tuna sandwiches (70 g tuna, 4 slices bread)<br>salad with 1 tbsp olive/walnut/flaxseed oil<br>2 plums or other fresh fruit |
| **afternoon snack:** | 1 meal replacement bar<br>grapes or other fresh fruit |
| **evening meal:** | chicken (85 g), vegetable and cashew stir fry<br>85 g (dry weight) whole grain rice |
| **evening snack:** | 4 rice cakes with 4 tbsp cottage cheese<br>pear and kiwi fruit (or other fresh fruit) |

**daily totals:**
2750 calories; 125 g protein; 436 g carbohydrate; 56 g fat

# eat more frequently

Dividing your food into several small meals provides a near-constant influx of protein, carbohydrates and other nutrients. Protein helps repair muscle fibres and carbohydrate keeps your blood sugar levels up, which prevents muscle breakdown while increasing the formation of glycogen.

Get into the habit of eating every 3–4 hours. Going 5 or more hours between meals makes you more likely to store fat, burn muscle and promote fluctuating blood sugar levels, leaving you tired and weak.

Depending on your calorie needs and your goals, these meals should contain between 300–700 calories.

## case study

Footballer and fitness instructor, David Eatock, used to eat three (really) big meals a day, topping up with lots of bread. The problem was he felt so full up afterwards that he had little motivation for hard training. After analysing his eating pattern, I advised him to eat six smaller meals spread throughout the day and snack on fresh fruit if he felt hungry. He also includes a meal replacement shake after his workouts, too. David now reports having heaps more energy for his weights workouts and finds that he recovers much faster between workouts.

## carbs for fuel

Carbohydrate is just as important as protein for muscle building. It is the major fuel you use for lifting weights. During an intense workout, you may deplete more than half of your glycogen reserves in your muscles. The only way you can re-stock your glycogen is by eating carbohydrate. Without it, you'll feel weak, fatigued and unable to lift weights heavy enough to stimulate muscle growth.

When you eat plenty of carbohydrates, your glycogen stores fill up and encourage your body to hold onto protein and build new muscle. When you skimp on carbs, your glycogen stores empty quickly, causing protein to be burned for fuel and thus not available for muscle building, so you'll end up smaller not bigger.

Carbohydrate also raises insulin levels in the blood. Insulin is an anabolic hormone, driving protein and carbohydrates into the muscle cells, encouraging muscle repair and growth.

## so how much carbohydrate do you need?

If you train with weights 3–5 times a week, aim to have between 5–7 g carbohydrate per kg of body weight per day (see pages 25–26). Endurance athletes and those who train more frequently may need as much as 8 g carbohydrate per kg of body weight per day.

Your carbohydrate needs will vary according to your physical demands and your goals. For example, if you are fairly inactive during the day – say, sitting at a computer or driving – your energy and carbohydrate needs will be much lower than those of an athlete or a builder, so your intake of carbohydrates should be lower.

On average, a 70 kg weight trainer will probably need between 350–490 g of carbohydrate daily. But hard gainers with low levels of body fat may need to add more. If you have been at a muscle-building plateau for a month or so, increase your carbohydrate intake by 50 g a day for a few days, and then another 50 g until you start adding muscle.

## strawberry smoothie

*This delicious smoothie provides a balanced combination of protein and carbohydrate, which makes it a perfect post-workout drink. Strawberries are packed with vitamin C – just seven strawberries give your daily requirements (60 mg) – and other powerful antioxidants. You can substitute other fresh or frozen berries for the strawberries if you prefer.*

**makes 2 drinks**

6 ice cubes
225 g (8 oz) ripe strawberries
1 banana
250 ml (8 fl oz) or 2 x 125 ml pots low fat natural yoghurt
90 ml (3 fl oz) skimmed milk
½ teaspoon (2.5 ml) vanilla extract

- Place the ice cubes in the goblet of a smoothie maker, blender or food processor and process until slushy.
- Add the strawberries, banana, yoghurt, milk and vanilla and process until smooth. Chill in the fridge or drink immediately.

## CARBS – WHEN TO EAT THEM

When in the day you should eat your carbohydrates depends on your goals. Hard gainers with low body fat should spread their carbs evenly throughout the day and eat within a couple of hours of going to bed, since their fast metabolism may otherwise put them in negative calorie balance while sleeping.

Those wishing to reduce body fat may be better off eating more carbs earlier in the day and around their workouts (see Chapters 2, 3 and 4) when their energy demands are greatest. Research at the University of Texas at Austin has found that eating carbs combined with protein after a workout is the best way to stimulate muscle growth (see also page 46). It promotes faster glycogen replacement as well as higher levels of growth hormone. Aim to have a protein- carbohydrate snack within an hour of finishing your workout.

# seven eating tips for hard gainers

**1** Schedule meals and snacks into your daily routine.

**2** Never skip meals no matter how busy you are.

**3** Increase your meal frequency – eat at least five or six meals or snacks daily.

**4** Eat regularly and avoid gaps longer than four hours.

**5** Have nutritious but calorie-dense snacks (see below) rather than high fat or sugary snacks.

**6** Boost the calorie and nutritional content of your meals without adding extra bulk using honey, dried fruit, nuts, peanut butter or milk.

**7** To prevent bloating, try liquid meals, such as milk shakes, smoothies, juices and meal replacement shakes and bars.

# will supplements help me build muscle?

There are countless supplements claiming to enhance muscle growth but you should be cautious of extravagant claims that sound too good to be true. The chances are they don't work. Many nutritional supplements are lacking safety data and scientific proof and some have even been found to contain illegal substances!

Before considering taking any supplement, you need to look carefully at what you are eating and make sure first that your meals are healthy and balanced. Only once you are confident that your diet and training programme is well balanced, should you think about supplements. You may benefit from the following (see Chapter 6):

- multivitamin and mineral supplements
- meal replacement supplements
- protein supplements
- creatine
- glutamine
- HMB.

## high calorie snacks for hard gainers

- nuts
- dried fruit – raisins, dates, apricots, mangos and peaches
- milkshake
- smoothie
- yoghurt
- sandwich, bagel, roll, pitta or muffin
- cereal or breakfast bar*
- flapjack
- meal replacement shake
- nutrition or protein bar

* without hydrogenated fat

## post-workout snacks for building muscle

- yoghurt
- meal replacement shake
- milkshake
- tuna sandwich
- meal replacement or nutrition bar
- rice cakes and cottage cheese

# eating for running

If running is your main fitness activity, whether on the treadmill or the road, you'll need to know exactly what and how much you should eat to help you run faster and longer. Chapters 1–4 give you much of the background you need to put together your eating plan, but this chapter gives you extra eating tips for running. It deals with problems that are common amongst runners and provides you with a smart pre-race eating strategy to help you get ahead of the competition.

## how many calories?

Running burns a lot of calories – the exact number depends on your speed, the incline, and your weight. For example, on the flat, you could burn more than 1000 calories per hour if you weigh 70 kg. Here are some average values for people of various weights at various speeds running on level ground.

| speed | cals/ kg/hr | 60 kg | 65 kg | 70 kg | 75 kg | 80 kg |
|---|---|---|---|---|---|---|
| jog (8.3 km/h or 5.2 mph) | 8.1 | 486 | 527 | 567 | 608 | 648 |
| fast (12.0 km/h or 7.5 mph) | 12.5 | 750 | 813 | 875 | 938 | 1000 |
| hard (16.0 km/h or 10.0 mph) | 15.1 | 906 | 982 | 1057 | 1133 | 1208 |

Use these values and the calculations on page 56 to help you work out how many calories you should eat each day. If you run for 30 minutes daily, you'll probably need between 2500 and 3500 calories daily. An elite endurance runner would need between 3500 and 5000 calories per day.

**Will I use more calories over a given distance if I run fast or slowly?**

If you were to cover, say, five miles in 30 minutes, you would burn the same calories as you would jogging the same distance in 45 minutes. In fact, the calorie burn would be the same even if you walked the distance.

The difference comes once you have stopped. Your metabolic rate will stay higher for several hours after intense exercise whereas the metabolic boost will be far lower after moderate activity. This means that you burn more calories after you have finished a fast run than after a slow run.

## power punch

*This energising drink will replenish your glycogen stores after a tough run and boost your vitamin intake. Blueberries are terrific sources of immunity-boosting vitamin C and anthocyanins. The yoghurt provides body-building protein, calcium and B vitamins.*

**makes 2 drinks**

125 g (4 oz) blueberries
1 peach, stone removed and chopped
200 ml (7 fl oz) apple juice
150 ml (5 fl oz) yoghurt
8–10 ice cubes

• Put the blueberries, peaches, apple juice, yoghurt and ice cubes into a smoothie maker, blender or food processor and blend until smooth. Serve immediately.

## fuel up

Filling your glycogen stores before training will delay the onset of fatigue. As a bonus, the run will seem easier to complete when you have enough glycogen on board. Eating a daily diet containing 5–7 g carbohydrate per kg of body weight (that's 350–490 g for a 70 kg runner) will speed your recovery from daily runs.

## fuel on the run

If you run for longer than an hour, consuming carbohydrate – say in the form of a sports drink – provides your muscles with a ready supply of blood glucose for immediate energy, which spares glycogen stores and helps you to run better. In a study at Loughborough University, runners were given either a sports drink (containing 5.5 or 6.9 g carbohydrate per 100 ml) or water during the first 60 minutes of a run, then asked to run until they couldn't keep going any longer. Those who consumed the sports drink were able to run almost 12 minutes longer than those who drank only water.

## re-fuel

Replacing your glycogen stores after a run is crucial if you want to run well the next day. A 30 minute window exists after exercise when muscles are most receptive to carbohydrate. If you spend this time showering or rushing back to work, you'll delay your recovery and may not run so well the next day. Get into the habit of having a drink or snack containing carbohydrate and some protein (such as a meal replacement shake or bar) straight after a run. Studies at the University of Texas have shown that consuming carbohydrate within two hours of exercise, ideally with protein in a ratio of 3 to 1, speeds glycogen recovery. Other good choices are fruit with a glass of milk, a carton of yoghurt, a yoghurt drink or a homemade milkshake (see Chapter 4, pages 46–48 for further ideas.).

**I have no appetite after a run and don't feel like eating. Should I wait until I'm hungry or force myself to eat?**

A lot of runners find they have little appetite after training. Running (along with other types of intense exercise) elevates your temperature and diverts blood away from your digestive system, which in turn depresses your appetite. If you want to recover faster, or you run every day, you should consume some carbohydrate within the first 30 minutes after a run or, at the very least, within two hours. Try a liquid meal, such as a meal replacement shake, milkshake, smoothie or yoghurt drink. You'll feel better during your run the next day.

**I sometimes suffer from diarrhoea on long runs. What causes it and how can I prevent it?**

The runner's 'trots' or 'runs' is common among endurance runners. Studies have shown that as many as one in four marathon runners experience it. The most likely explanation is that your lower gut (colon) becomes starved of oxygen during long runs due to a reduced blood flow. Blood is diverted away from your gut to your muscles and your skin, where more blood is required. This can result in spasmodic contractions of the colon.

Being dehydrated would make the situation worse as your reduced blood volume means that even less blood is available to the gut. Your best strategy to prevent diarrhoea would be to drink plenty of water before and during your run. Make sure that you drink during the early stages. It's also a good idea to avoid eating high fibre foods, especially bran and whole grain cereals, pulses and dried fruit too close to the time of you run. These may loosen the stools and trigger bowel movements, a situation made worse by pre-race nerves. Caffeine and sorbitol sometimes have a laxative effect so you may also wish to avoid drinks and foods containing them. Keeping a food and training diary can help you work out which foods you can tolerate and which ones you need to steer clear of before a run.

**I often get cramps in my calves during a run. Is there anything I can eat or drink to stop this happening?**

Muscle cramps may be caused by several factors, including dehydration, increased body temperature and electrolyte (sodium/potassium) imbalance. Drink plenty of fluids before and during a run to offset dehydration. Sports drinks that contain sodium and potassium may help prevent cramps, alternatively try diluted fruit juice with a pinch of ordinary salt.

## sample meal plan for a runner

**breakfast:** 1 large bowl muesli or other wholegrain cereal
200 ml (⅓ pint) semi-skimmed milk
banana or apple
2 slices of wholegrain toast spread with 1 tbsp honey

**morning snack:** 1 yoghurt drink or power punch (see recipe on page 108)
2 kiwi fruit (or other vitamin C rich fruit)

**lunch:** turkey sandwich (2 slices wholewheat bread, 60 g sliced turkey)
salad with 1 tbsp olive/walnut/flaxseed oil
nectarine or plums

**afternoon snack:** 1 breakfast bar
1 portion fresh fruit

**evening meal:** grilled chicken breast (85 g)
1 large baked potato topped with 1 tbsp olive oil or hummus
large portion of carrots and broccoli
apple crumble with yoghurt

**daily totals:**
2580 calories; 400 g carbohydrate; 117 g protein; 68 g fat

If I have cereal or any other solid food before running, then my run turns into a running tour of south London's public toilets! I've experimented with various foods and drinks – sports drinks give me an upset stomach – but I run best on an empty stomach, drinking only water en route.

CATHERINE COMPTON, MARATHON RUNNER

# preparing for a race

After months of training, you now feel ready to enter a race. Congratulations! Preparing for a race – whether it's your first 5 k or a marathon – is a challenging but rewarding experience. Here's a pre-race nutrition strategy to help you perform at your very best on race day.

## a few weeks before

### step up your calorie intake

If you increase your weekly mileage or up your running pace, you'll need to match your calorie intake to your output. If you ran 10 miles a week before you began training for a race, and you increased this to 20 miles a week during race training, you will need to eat an extra 1400 calories a week (that's 200 extra calories a day). Fail to adjust your calorie intake and you risk a drop in your performance and losing muscle. Low muscle glycogen levels will make training runs feel harder and may reduce your immunity.

### get into the snack habit

The easiest way to fit in the extra calories is by dividing your food intake into regular small meals or snacks. A steady calorie and nutrient intake will help maintain normal blood sugar levels, improve glycogen refuelling and minimise fat storage. Carry healthy snacks, such as sports bars, fruit and nuts with you so you always have a quick source of good nutrition to hand.

### eat plenty of fruit and vegetables

These vitamin- and antioxidant-packed foods will boost your immunity and help counteract the extra free radicals produced during intense training. Eat at least five portions daily. The more intense the colour, the higher the antioxidant content.

### learn to drink on the run

If you don't already, you'll need to learn how to handle drinks on the run (see 'Drinking on the run' on page 114). Take frequent small sips to prevent overloading your stomach.

### test in training what you plan to do during the race

Practise grabbing cups and drinking on the move without spilling or choking. Find out which sports drink will be provided during the race and get used to it by trying it during training. If you choose energy gels or bars, practise eating these during training and drinking 125–250 ml water for each gel or bar.

**Despite doing a lot of running, I still have cellulite. Is it different from ordinary fat and is there a special diet I could follow to help get rid of it?**

You might be reassured to learn that cellulite affects 85% of all women and over 95% of women over 30. Even exercise fanatics can be plagued by it. Cellulite is simply fat. The reason it appears dimpled and puckered is that it lies very close to the skin's surface and is criss-crossed by weak collagen strands that don't do a very good job supporting the fat cells. This results in the characteristic bulging appearance of cellulite on your body. The reason women get it far more than men is the female hormone oestrogen, which favours fat storage on your thighs and bottom so women tend to put weight on in these areas. Inactivity and excess calories also play a big role in the formation of cellulite. But some experts believe that if you spend several hours a day sitting down, even if you run every day, the lymphatic system slows down, which results in poor drainage from the fat cells. That explains why even regular exercisers can get cellulite. A healthy but careful calorie consumption combined with exercise are the only proven ways to beat cellulite. There is no evidence that it's caused by 'toxins', nor that following a so-called detox diet reduces cellulite. However, cutting back on processed foods, sugar and fat will help reduce cellulite because you will have eaten fewer calories.

## the week before the race

Your aim during the week before the race is to fill your muscles with the glycogen you'll need during the race. Starting with high glycogen levels will help you to keep going longer before you get tired.

### *taper your training*

For the last few days before the race, reduce your training intensity and duration and then rest for the last day or two.

## downsize your meals

You'll be training less as the week progresses, so you may need to drop your calorie intake a little. Do this by cutting out foods containing saturated fats and 'empty calories', such as confectionery, pastries, crisps and fast foods.

## carb up

Change the nutrient mix of your pre-race diet so you get more of your calories from carbohydrate (60–70%) and fewer from fat (less than 15–20%), the balance coming from protein. Remember it's the proportion of carbs not the total calories that needs to go up.

## eat little and often

Small frequent meals will be easier to digest and stop you feeling bloated. Avoid big meals and don't eat too much of any one food.

## slow burn

Choose low-glycaemic meals and foods, which will promote better glycogen storage. Carbs eaten with some protein or healthy fat (such as potatoes with chicken, pasta with fish, rice with tofu) give a longer slower energy release compared with carbs on their own.

## get bottle savvy

Keep well hydrated by drinking at least 2 litres per day.

---

### DRINKING ON THE RUN

It's not easy to drink on the run but by not drinking you risk dehydration and poor performance. Try the following options:

- hold a runner's drink bottle (available from running shops) in your hand. It will feel awkward at first but you'll soon get used to training with it
- Run 3–5 mile loops around your house, gym or car and stop off every time you pass to grab a drink
- take some money with you and plan your route to pass a shop where you can stop for a drink.

**CARBOHYDRATE LOADING**

Carbohydrate loading – increasing your glycogen stores above normal – will improve your performance during races lasting 90 minutes or longer. But it won't help you run faster in shorter runs. In fact, the heaviness associated with elevated glycogen stores may hinder your performance in 5 k or 10 k runs. In the first three days, eat a normal diet. During the three days before the event, eat a high carbohydrate diet providing 7–10 g carbohydrate per day. On the sixth day before the race run at a hard pace. On the following two days, run shorter distances at the same intensity. On the third and second day before the race, run only very short distances. On the day before the race, rest.

# the day before

By now, your muscle glycogen stores should be almost fully stocked and you should be feeling rested. Your goals for the day before your race are to top up your glycogen stores, stay well-hydrated and avoid any pitfalls that may jeopardise your performance the next day.

### graze

Eat little and often throughout the day. Choose high carbohydrate, low fat, moderate protein meals to avoid overburdening your digestive system.

### avoid feasting

It's not a good idea to over-indulge the night before a race as this can play havoc with your digestive system and keep you awake at night. You may feel sluggish the next day.

### stick with familiar foods

Eat only foods that you know agree with you and eat them in normal-sized amounts. Don't try anything new.

### avoid alcohol

It's a diuretic and, if you over-indulge, you may feel below par the next day.

## beware of the gas

Avoid gas-forming foods (or combinations of food) such as baked beans and other pulses, vegetables such as broccoli, Brussels sprouts and cauliflower, bran cereals and spicy foods the night before the race. They can make you feel uncomfortable.

## take to the bottle

Keep a water bottle handy so you remember to drink regularly throughout the day. This is especially important if you are travelling to the race venue on this day, as it's easy to forget to drink.

# on race day

By now, your muscle glycogen stores should be fully stocked and you should feel ready to go! All that remains to be done before the race is to top-up your liver glycogen stores at breakfast time (liver glycogen is normally depleted during the overnight fast), replace any fluids lost overnight and keep your blood sugar level steady.

## eat early

Remember it takes 3–4 hours for food to digest so schedule your pre-race meal early. If your race starts at 9 am, have breakfast at 6 am.

## eat light

Aim for 25–50 g of carbohydrate for each hour before the start of the race, depending on your body weight and the race duration (see 'pre-race meals' below). Carbohydrate-rich foods, such as porridge, cereal, toast and fruit are good choices. Include a little protein or healthy fat to reduce the glycaemic response (see page 13) and give a slow steady energy release. If you can't eat

**On the day of a race, I have a good breakfast, say scrambled egg on two slices of brown toast, 3 or 4 hours before. I also take a little stash of snacks with me for after the finish. I like to have a quick hit of sugar, like a cereal bar or a couple slices of toast and jam.**

SUSIE WHALLEY, 4 TIME LONDON MARATHON RUNNER

because of pre-race nerves, have an extra bedtime snack the day before, or try a liquid meal (e.g. meal replacement shake, milkshake, smoothie, yoghurt drink) for breakfast, which will empty from your stomach faster than solid food.

## drink before you race

Drink at least 400–600 ml of water, a sports drink or diluted fruit juice (1 part juice to 1 or 2 parts water) about 2 hours before the race, then top up with a smal cupful just before the race.

### pre-race meals

*Accompany the following with 1–2 cups (150–300 ml) of water or diluted fruit juice (1 part juice, 1 or 2 parts water)*

- porridge with raisins and honey
- cereal with milk and bananas
- toast with jam and a milky drink
- pancakes or waffles with honey
- meal replacement shake
- meal replacement bar
- protein shake and fresh fruit
- yoghurt and fresh fruit
- fruit smoothie
- yoghurt drink

## during the race

### drink every 20 minutes

Begin drinking within the first 30 minutes to minimise dehydration instead of trying to rehydrate yourself later. Aim to drink 150–350 ml every 15 to 20 minutes or as much as you can cope with. Use whichever drinking method you trained with. Don't rely on thirst, as this is a poor indicator of your fluid needs. Be extra diligent in hot and humid weather.

## slow down through the fluid stations

Walk or slow down to drink at least a cupful at every fluid station. If you try to run you'll end up spilling most of the drink. Squeezing the cup into a funnel makes it easier to drink. Don't be tempted to miss out the early fluid stations to gain valuable time – dehydration later on will slow you down even more.

## choose the right drink

If there's a choice, select plain water for races lasting less than an hour and sports drinks for longer events. Stick with whatever you used in training and don't try anything new.

### Is it possible to drink too much water?

During long endurance events such as marathons or ironman triathlons, overhydrating yourself by constantly drinking water may dilute your blood so that your sodium levels fall, a condition known as hyponatraemia. Although it is quite rare it is potentially fatal. USA Track & Field caution against drinking huge amounts of water in events lasting longer than 4 hours and advise instead being guided by your thirst and drinking sports drinks with sodium. But for most runners, there is a bigger risk of dehydration than overhydration.

# after the race

Congratulations! You made it past the finishing line. But your nutrition strategy isn't over yet as you still have to replenish your fluid losses and refill your depleted glycogen stores. This is especially important if you plan to be active the next day or even if you want to move around without difficulty tomorrow!

## drink, drink, and drink

For every half-kilo (1 lb) of bodyweight you have lost, you need to drink 750 ml of fluid. Try to drink around 500 ml in the first 30 minutes and keep gulping every 5 or 10 minutes until you have reached your target.

If you pass only a small volume of dark yellow urine, or if you are headachy and nauseous, then you need to keep drinking. If you are dehydrated, then sports drinks or diluted juice (with a pinch of added salt) are your best options.

## grab a snack

Choose a high carbohydrate snack and aim to consume 1 g of carbohydrate per kg of bodyweight (70 g for a 70 kg runner) within the first 30 minutes. It doesn't matter whether it's food or drink – have whatever feels right (see the box 'post-race snacks' below).

## keep eating

Continue eating a similar-sized snack every two hours until your proper meal. This will promote faster recovery. It takes at least 24 hours to replenish glycogen stores after a short run, but up to 7 days after a marathon.

## don't pig-out!

Resist the temptation to eat burgers, fries, kebabs and other fatty or spicy foods after the race. They will sit heavily your stomach, slow your recovery and leave you feeling bloated and sluggish. Stick to easily digested meals, such as pasta with tomato sauce, jacket potatoes with tuna or cottage cheese, chicken sandwiches, a bagel with a little cheese, vegetable and tofu stir-fries, or noodles with prawns.

## post-race snacks

*Accompany the following with 1–2 cups (150–300 ml) of water or diluted fruit juice (1 part juice, 1 or 2 parts water)*

- cereal bar or sports bar
- meal replacement shake
- yoghurt drink
- fresh fruit
- dried fruit and nuts
- fruit cake or malt loaf (see recipe opposite)
- jam sandwich, roll or bagel

# fantastic fruit loaf

*This is virtually fat-free and is the perfect refuelling snack after a run. You can substitute any of the dried fruits suggested in the recipe.*

125 g (4 oz) dried apricots, chopped
125 g (4 oz) dried apples, chopped
125 g (4 oz) dried mango pieces
300 ml (½ pint) orange or apple juice

225 g (8 oz) self-raising flour
125 g (4 oz) soft dark brown sugar
1 egg

- Place the dried fruit in a bowl and cover with the fruit juice. Leave to soak for two hours.
- Lightly oil a 900 g (2 lb) loaf tin. Pre-heat the oven to 180°C/350°F/Gas mark 4.
- Place all of the ingredients in a large bowl and mix together well.
- Spoon the mixture into the prepared tin and level the surface.
- Bake for about 1 hour or until cooked through. You may need to cover the tin with foil after 30 minutes to prevent over-browning.
- Allow the cake to cool in the tin for 15 minutes before turning out on to a wire rack.

## How can I avoid 'hitting the wall' during a marathon?

'Hitting the wall' occurs when your muscles run out of glycogen and your blood sugar level plummets. At this stage, you're in real trouble. Your body needs some carbohydrate to burn fat, but when there are no carbs your brain and nervous system can't work properly. This makes exercise difficult if not impossible. You may feel weak, dizzy, nauseous and disorientated. To avoid hitting the wall consume carbohydrate at regular intervals during your run, aiming to have 30–60 g carbohydrate for every hour of exercise. That's equivalent to drinking 500–1000 ml of sports drink (containing 60 g carbohydrate/ litre) each hour. Take regular sips and start drinking early as it takes about 30 minutes for the carbohydrate to reach your active muscles. This will help to keep your blood sugar levels steady and fuel your active muscles during that last stage of the race.

**I always seem to come down with a cold a couple of days after a long run or race. How can I prevent this happening?**

It's ironic that regular moderate exercise boosts your immunity, but intense workouts actually suppress the immune system and increase your chances of catching a cold. Scientists at Appalachian State University, North Carolina, believe that that this is due to the rise of stress hormones during a tough workout, such as a long run. During this 'open window' of lowered immunity – which can last from 3–72 hours – viruses and bacteria can get a foothold. Here are some tips that will cut your chances of infection:

**1 Eat five**: Getting the five-day recommended portions of fruit and vegetables will keep your immune system in good shape during training. These foods are packed with antioxidant nutrients, which fight harmful free radicals, support your immune system and protect your body from viruses.

**2 Swig a drink**: According to Appalachian University research, consuming carbohydrate (supplying 30–60 g carbohydrate per hour) during a race boosts the immune system. It does this by preventing risky dips in blood sugar. A low blood sugar level signals the body to release more stress hormones (such as cortisol), which greatly suppresses your immune function. So, sipping a sports drink, diluted juice or taking energy gels with water during a race may just give you the edge to keep colds and sore throats at bay.

**3 Pop a pill**: Try taking antioxidant or vitamin C supplements a few weeks before your race. One study at the University of Cape Town found that antioxidant supplements (vitamin C/ vitamin E/beta-carotene) taken 21 days before the race halved the number of post race infections.

**4 Take a nap**: Getting sufficient rest after a race helps alleviate the stress to your immune system, making a cold less likely.

# eating for cycling

Whether you cycle to work, cycle for fitness or enjoy the more serious challenges of long rides and races, eating smart will help you cycle faster and longer. Firstly you should familiarise yourself with the information contained in Chapters 1–4 so you'll know how to construct a good eating plan for your training rides. This chapter gives you additional tips on eating for cycling as well as answering the most common nutrition questions asked by cyclists. It also provides a pre-race eating and drinking strategy to help you make it to the finish without 'bonking' (running out of energy' like 'hitting the wall' in running)!

## how many calories?

Cycling demands a lot of energy from your body. The number of calories you burn cycling depends on your speed, the terrain, your weight and how long you are in the saddle. For example, cycling at a leisurely pace (11.3 km/h or 7 mph) burns 298 calories per hour if you weigh 70 kg, while racing (25.8 km/h or 16 mph) burns around 710 calories per hour. The table below shows you approximately how many calories you burn per hour at various speeds.

| speed | cals/ kg/hr | 60 kg | 65 kg | 70 kg | 75 kg | 80 kg |
|-------|------|-------|-------|-------|-------|-------|
| leisure (11.3 km/h or 7 mph) | 4.26 | 256 | 277 | 298 | 320 | 341 |
| hard (16.1 km/h or 10 mph) | 6.42 | 385 | 417 | 449 | 482 | 514 |
| racing (25.8 km/h or 16 mph) | 10.14 | 608 | 659 | 710 | 761 | 811 |

Your daily calorie needs also depend on your weight, as well as your muscle mass, daily activity level and training frequency. To get an idea of how many calories you should be eating, see page 56. If you cycle for an hour daily, you'll probably need between 2500 and 3500 calories daily. A professional cyclist would need between 4000 and 6500 calories per day.

# tips for all cyclists

## eat the right fuel

A carbohydrate-rich diet is essential for all cyclists. Carbs are turned into glycogen in your muscles, which then fuels your training. When your muscle glycogen stores are high, your training rides will feel easier, you'll be able to keep going longer and faster before getting tired. If you cycle for less than 2 hours per day, you'll probably need to eat 5–7 g of carbohydrate per kg of bodyweight per day (that's 350–490 g for a 70 kg cyclist). If you cycle up to 4 hours daily, you'll need more like 6–8 g of carbohydrate per kg of bodyweight per day (that's 420–560 g for a 70 kg cyclist).

## fuel up in the saddle

For rides longer than 40 km, you will certainly need something other than water to keep your energy levels up. Take a supply of sports drinks (or fruit juice diluted 50/50 with water) and/or a carbohydrate-rich snacks (such as energy bars, gels, bananas or breakfast bars) with you. You'll need to begin fuelling within the first 30 minutes as it takes a further 30 minutes for those carbs to reach your active muscles. If you eat solid food, drink water rather than sports drinks, aiming for 500–1000 ml per hour (depending on the heat, humidity and your intensity). That's equivalent to one or two standard (500 ml) water bottles.

Studies have shown that consuming extra carbohydrate on rides lasting longer than 90 minutes increases endurance and performance during a race. Aim to consume around 30–60 g of carbohydrate per hour, that's between 120 and 240 calories.

**HOW TO STAY IN THE SADDLE LONGER**

In a study at the University of Texas at Austin, cyclists were given either a sports drink (containing 10% carbohydrate), an energy bar with water or artificially-flavoured water (placebo). Those who consumed some form of carbohydrate managed to keep going 21 minutes and 30 seconds longer before reaching exhaustion than those who only drank flavoured water. The reason? The extra carbs helped fuel the cyclists' muscles, reducing the dependency on glycogen. After 3 hours in the saddle, the cyclists sipping the sports drink or eating food had 35% more glycogen than those who had no carbs.

## Stash your food

You have the advantage over other endurance athletes in that you can carry fluids and food on the bike frame or in jersey pockets. Also, it's easier to eat solid foods, as you're not bouncing around. Learning to eat during cycling without swerving can be tricky at first (see 'How to eat and drink in the saddle').

## Drink in the saddle

Many cyclists under-estimate their fluid losses and fail to drink enough. Wind-chill and rapid evaporation of sweat can give you the false sense that you're not losing much fluid. Even if you don't feel hot or sweaty, you could be dehydrated so you still need to drink. Start drinking in the first 30 minutes of your ride. Take frequent gulps, aiming for about 125 ml every 15–20 minutes.

## Try a sports drink

Sports drinks supply fluid and carbohydrate at the same time. Most commercial drinks supply 20–40 g carbohydrate per standard 500 ml water bottle (80–160 calories). You'll need one or two standard bottles per hour. Be warned that some brands can sit heavy in the stomach during hard rides – you may find them easier to tolerate when diluted with extra water. You'll need to experiment to find the drink strength that suits you best. Try making up powdered drinks with extra water if necessary or take a bottle of sports drink and a bottle of water, drinking both in turn.

## Refuel

The best time to eat carbo-hydrate is within 30 minutes after a ride. There exists a 30 minute to 2 hour window when glycogen is re-stocked about one and a half times faster than normal. The sooner you can get carbo-hydrate to your muscles, the faster you will be able to recover. If you have a high-carbohydrate snack, ideally with a little protein (in a ratio of about 1 g of protein to 3 g of carbohydrate), as soon as you have showered, you will be able to cycle better the next day and feel generally more energetic. If you leave a longer gap before eating, it will take you longer to recover and your legs won't feel as fresh the next day.

> I cannot eat solid food before I cycle as it makes me feel uncomfortable throughout my ride. Instead, I drink my home-made sports drink – fruit juice diluted with water – to keep up my energy levels. During long rides, I take bananas and breakfast bars to help me keep going.
>
> ANDY JACKSON, COMPETITIVE CYCLIST

## how to eat and drink in the saddle

- on long rides, wearing a specially designed pack that contains a plastic bladder (such as a camel pack) will allow you to drink without having to take your hands off the handlebars. You can carry larger volumes of drink without needing to stop off to refill your bottle.

- in hot weather, add ice cubes to your drink or freeze half the bottle (or camel pack) overnight and top it up before you get on your bike.

- you can carry small snacks in the pockets of your jersey.

- you can open your bars and undo packets before you set off so the food is easy to get at with one hand during your ride.

- peel fruit and wrap in foil for easy access.

- wrap dried fruit and biscuits in foil or small re-sealable plastic bags.

- soft textured bars may be wrapped around your handlebars for easy access.

- practise riding without holding onto the handlebars so that you can balance more easily while you eat and drink.

## what to eat in the saddle

For rides longer than 40 km you will need food to replenish your energy supplies. Make sure you drink plenty of water too.

- energy bars
- cereal bars, fruit bars and breakfast bars*
- energy gels
- bananas and other fruit
- malt loaf or fruit cake
- raisins or sultanas
- fig rolls

*Choose varieties that contain no hydrogenated fat and less than 5 g total fat.

**WILL FLAT COLA HELP ME KEEP GOING LONGER?**

A lot of sportspeople (particularly cyclists) swear by drinking flat cola during long hard workouts and races. Much of the claimed benefits are based on hearsay handed down from one competitor to another. The truth is that cola possesses no special performance-enhancing quality – it is a simply a sugary drink, containing around 11 g – that's 2 teaspoons – of sugar per 100 ml. It can give you a quick energy boost, but it won't hydrate you fast as it is too concentrated to empty from the stomach quickly. You'll get a similar sugar 'hit' from an isotonic sports drink, diluted juice, energy gel or solid food taken with a drink of water. Cola also supplies caffeine, but you'd need to drink around 1 litre of it to get an endurance benefit. If you must drink cola, alternate it with water, but remember that its high sugar and acid content are harmful to your teeth.

## apple, pear and orange juice

*Perfect after a long ride, this drink will replenish fluid losses as well as refuelling your carbohydrate stores. It's wonderfully refreshing and provides plenty of vitamin C, potassium and magnesium.*

**makes 1 drink**
1 eating apple
1 ripe pear
2 oranges
A few ice cubes

You will need a juicer for this recipe. Roughly chop the apple and pear into manageable pieces. Peel the oranges and divide the flesh into segments. Juice the fruit and pour into glasses. Add the ice cubes.

*see note on juicing and juicers on page 31*

# preparing for a long ride or race

What you eat and drink in the weeks and days before a race or long ride makes a big difference to your performance. Start eating smart, as early in your preparations as possible – this will help you train smarter – and then fine tune your diet during the last week before the event.

## a few weeks before

*eat more!*

As you increase your weekly mileage or step up your training intensity, you'll need extra calories to fuel your body. For example, an extra 4 hours in the saddle each week burns around 1800 extra calories if you weigh 70 kg. Check the box on page 123 ('How many calories?') for an idea of how many extra calories you are burning. If you don't make any adjustment to your overall calorie intake, you risk losing body fat as well as muscle. Notice how many competitive cyclists who race week after week look drawn and 'wasted' during the competitive season. If you need to shed some body fat, the extra training coupled with a balanced intake of carbohydrate, protein and fat should result in a loss of around half a kilo (1 lb) a week.

## sample meal plan for a cyclist

**breakfast:** 1 toasted bagel or muffin
home-made milkshake or meal replacement
drink
oranges or kiwi fruit

**morning snack:** 1 cereal bar or flapjack
nectarine or peach

**lunch:** 1 large baked potato
baked beans with 2 tbsp grated cheese
salad with 1 tbsp olive/walnut/flaxseed oil
1 carton yoghurt

**afternoon snack:** 1 smoothie or 2 portions of fresh fruit
1 energy bar

**evening meal:** baked or grilled fish (85 g)
portion of cooked wholegrain rice
large portion of broccoli and cauliflower
1 bowl of rice pudding with strawberries
(or other fresh fruit)

**daily totals:**
2550 calories; 400 g carbohydrate; 104 g protein; 70 g fat

## *eat frequently*

You'll need to eat a lot of food to meet your calorie, carbohydrate and protein needs. Divide your food into three meals and two or three snacks. Eating regularly throughout the day encourages better glycogen refuelling, less fat storage and more constant energy levels.

## *don't forget protein*

A lot of endurance cyclists focus on carbohydrate but forget about protein but fat. While carbohydrate is important for fuelling your muscles, you also need protein to repair muscle fibres broken down during long hard rides. If you skimp on protein, you may lose muscle. During hard training, some protein, as well as carbohydrate and fat, is used as fuel and can make up as much as 15% of the calorie mix. You need 1.2–1.4 g per kg bodyweight daily, that's 84–98 g if you weigh 70 kg. So include a portion (about the size of your fist) of lean protein with each meal – chicken, fish, lean meat, cottage cheese, tofu or quorn.

## get fresh!

Eat at least five portions of fresh fruit and vegetables each day. They provide antioxidants, which not only boost your immunity but also may help counteract some of the harmful effects of pollutants you breathe in during road rides. Pollutants from traffic fumes and smog increase the number of free radicals that your body has to deal with. Left

**If you are likely to be racing at an unusual time, say early in the morning, change your eating times to reflect this up to a week beforehand. This way, your body will find it easier to exercise at the new time and you'll slip into an eating pattern that suits your exercise schedule.**

JOHN BREWER, DIRECTOR OF HUMAN PERFORMANCE AT LILLESHALL NATIONAL SPORTS CENTRE

unchecked, they could increase your risk of certain cancers and heart disease in later life, increase muscle soreness and lower your immunity. By stepping up your intake of antioxidant-rich foods, you'll bolster your body's natural defences against these free radicals. Choose a wide variety of fruit and vegetables – the more intensely coloured the higher the antioxidant potential. Blueberries, blackberries, strawberries, spinach, red peppers and Brussels sprouts are richest in antioxidants.

## learn to eat and drink in the saddle

If you don't already, you'll need to practice drinking from a water bottle or eating snacks while riding. Work out how to keep your balance without swerving while you drink or eat with one hand. Most cyclists move one hand to the centre of the handlebars (see page 126).

## practice your race strategy in training

Whatever you plan to do during the race, rehearse it in training. Practice drinking from a water bottle. Or if you plan to use a camel pack (see page 126) in the event, use it during your training rides. Experiment with different foods (see 'What to eat in the saddle' page 127) to find out the types and amounts that suit you best. Research the foods and drinks to be provided at the stations so you can test them out beforehand. Alternatively, take your own supplies.

## the week before

What you eat and drink during the week before your long ride or race can make a big difference to your performance. You goals are to maximise your muscle glycogen stores and keep yourself well hydrated.

### train less

Taper your training gradually. For the last few days of the week you should be cutting the time spent in the saddle by half and then resting completely for the last day or two. If you don't reduce your training you risk using the carbohydrate you're eating to fuel your training rides instead of stockpiling it for the big event.

### carb up

Increase the amount of carbohydrate in your diet and reduce the fat calories in a corresponding amount. Tipping the balance a little more in favour of carbs (roughly 60–70% carbohydrate calories) will boost your glycogen levels and give you more fuel for the event. Tapering your training along with increasing your carb intake can increase your endurance by as much as 20%.

### drink plenty

Make sure that you drink at least 2–3 litres per day. Dehydration is cumulative so if you failed to drink enough over a few days, the effects carry over, which means that you could be dehydrated on the day of the race.

### avoid big meals

Eating too much in one meal will reduce the amount of glycogen stored and increase the chances of fat gain. Try to keep to regular meal times during the final week to avoid stomach upsets.

## the day before

The day before the race is your final chance to top up those muscle glycogen stores. It's also important to keep yourself hydrated and avoid eating or drinking anything that may jeopardise your performance.

### eat small

Divide your food into smaller more frequent amounts than usual meals. Grazing will maximise glycogen storage without making you feel bloated and 'heavy'.

### don't try any new foods

The last thing you want before a race is a stomach upset so play it safe by sticking to familiar foods. Choose fairly plain foods, such as fish and rice or baked potato with cottage cheese, and avoid spicy and salty foods such as crisps, takeaways, ready-made sauces and ready-meals.

### keep drinking

Drink plenty of fluids throughout the day. Your urine should be pale or almost clear.

### avoid windy days!

Steer clear of gas-forming foods, such as baked beans, lentils and other pulses, cauliflower, Brussels sprouts, bran cereals and spicy foods. Eating them could give you an uncomfortable ride the next day!

### don't party

Do not over-indulge the evening before your race. A large meal – even if it's high in carbohydrate – could make you feel sluggish the next day. If you must drink alcohol, restrict yourself to a maximum of two units, otherwise you risk dehydration and a hangover on race day. Better still, avoid alcohol altogether.

## on race day

On the day of the race, your muscle glycogen levels should be fully stocked and you should be feeling full of energy. But what you eat just before your race is crucial too. Consuming carbs, particularly before longer rides and

## pre-race meals

- cereal with dried fruit and milk
- scrambled egg on toast
- porridge with fruit
- toasted bagels or muffins and milky drink
- meal replacement shake with fruit
- homemade milkshake
- smoothie made with fruit and yoghurt

races, provides energy for hard working muscles. They will replenish the store of glycogen in your liver and keep up your blood sugar levels.

### eat a good breakfast

Eat your pre-race meal 2–4 hours before the start of your race otherwise you may suffer from terrible stomach cramps during the race. This is because your digestive system has a reduced blood flow during the race, which makes it very difficult to digest large meals. Have a moderate-sized carbohydrate-based breakfast that's also low in fat and contains some protein. Aim for 150–200 g of carbohydrate before a long ride. For short rides under 2 hours, you may need only 75–150 g. If you find it difficult to eat solid food when you're feeling nervous, try a liquid meal instead (see box 'Pre-race meals' above). Skipping that pre-race meal may leave you low in energy during the final stages.

### go easy on the fibre!

Steer clear of bran and high-fibre cereals, especially if you are feeling nervous. Cereal fibre may loosen the stools and cause more bowel movements than normal. Select foods that are fairly low in fibre, such as white toast instead of brown, cornflakes instead of bran flakes.

### drink

Make sure that you are properly hydrated by drinking 400–600 ml of water, a sports drink or diluted fruit juice (1 part juice to 1 or 2 parts water) about 2 hours before the race. Your urine should be a very pale yellow colour by the start time. It's also wise to top up with a further cupful just before you set off.

## drink every 15–20 minutes

Start drinking early, ideally in the first 15–20 minutes. Your goal then is to continue drinking little and often, aiming for 150–350 ml every 15 to 20 minutes. Remember that wind-chill and rapid evaporation of sweat can mask feelings of dehydration. Don't wait until you feel thirsty, as this is a poor indicator of your fluid needs.

## drink right

Drink whatever you used in training. As a rule of thumb, water is fine for 40 km races or rides lasting 60–90 minutes; sports drinks are better for longer races. But don't try anything different – even it's freely provided by the race organisers – in case it doesn't agree with you under race conditions.

## fuel in the saddle

For rides longer than 90 minutes you will need food or a sports drink to keep up your blood sugar levels. Try to consume 750–1000 ml an hour. Or try energy gels, bars or fruit with plenty of water. Eat little and often to save your digestive system having to work too hard.

## eat when the going gets easy

It's easier to eat and drink when you're riding on the flat and in a straight line, as climbing, descending and cornering demand your full concentration. Take advantage of the food served at the rest stops but don't eat anything you haven't used in training.

### HOW CAN I AVOID THE 'BONK'?

The 'bonk' is a common problem. It happens when you have used up the glycogen in your muscles and liver and have no energy left. To avoid this, drink sports drinks or eat high-carbohydrate snacks regularly during the ride. Try energy bars, bananas, energy gels, and cereal or fruit bars. Aim to consume 30–60 g carbohydrate per hour, that's one or two bars (depending on the size) or a couple of gel sachets or 2–4 bananas or 500–1000 ml of an isotonic sports drink (depending on the strength) or fruit juice diluted with 1 or 2 parts water.

## after the race

It's a great sense of accomplishment when you have completed the race and crossed the finish line. Before you load up your bike and start back home though, start rehydrating and refuelling your body. Recovery needs to begin now otherwise you could wake up tomorrow feeling weak and very sore.

### recovery snacks

*Accompany the following with 1–2 cups (150–300 ml) of water or diluted fruit juice (1 part juice, 1 or 2 parts water)*

- fruit and yoghurt
- flapjack (see recipe page 137)
- cereal bar, sports bar or breakfast bar
- fruit cake or malt loaf
- fruit buns or scones
- sandwich or bagel with light filing, e.g. turkey, jam, thin cheese slices
- meal replacement shake
- milkshake
- dried fruit and nuts

### *hit the bottle*

Drink plenty of water. As a guide, have a standard (500 ml) water bottle as soon as practical, ideally within the first 30 minutes, then keep drinking small regular amounts until your urine is pale in colour. Again, don't rely on thirst as this doesn't tell you whether you are properly rehydrated. If you are dehydrated, a sports drink or diluted juice with a pinch of added salt will deliver fluid faster and the sodium they contain helps your body retain the fluid better.

### *have a bar*

Have a carbohydrate-rich snack within the first 30 minutes (when blood flow to your muscles is greater and the muscles are more receptive to carbs). This will help re-build your glycogen stores. Choose a snack that provides around 1 g of carbohydrate per kg of bodyweight. For example, if you weigh 70 kg, you need to eat 70 g of carbohydrate immediately after the race. Try a sports drink or nutrition (sports) bar.

## chow down

Follow your post-race snack with a carbohydrate-rich meal within two hours. Including a small portion of lean protein will help replenish glycogen faster as well as help with muscle repair. Try rice with chicken, pasta with tomato sauce and cheese, a jacket potato with tuna or baked beans on toast.

## pass on the fry-up

It's tempting to head for the nearest greasy spoon café, burger van or fast food restaurant after a race. But fried, fatty or spicy foods will only sit heavily in your stomach at this time, impeding your recovery. Opt for lighter meals and save the greasy stuff for later on if you must!

# apple and date flapjacks

*These easy flapjacks make a perfect refuelling snack. They provide plenty of slow-release carbohydrate, B vitamins, vitamin C and iron. Pop these in your jersey pocket for a tasty post-race treat.*

**makes 16 flapjacks** 225 g (8 oz) butter or olive oil margarine
225 g (8 oz) soft light brown sugar
2 tbsp (30 ml) golden syrup
350 g (12 oz) porridge oats
1 sp (5 ml) ground cinnamon
2 eating apples, peeled, cored and sliced
200 g (7 oz) dates, roughly chopped

- Pre-heat the oven to 180°C/ 350°F/Gas mark 4. Lightly oil a 15 x 30 cm (6 x 12 in) tin.

- Put the butter or margarine, sugar and golden syrup in a pan and heat gently, stirring occasionally, until the butter has melted. Remove from the heat.

- Stir in the porridge oats and cinnamon.

- Put the prepared apples and dates in a separate pan with 2 tbsp (30 ml) water and cook over a medium heat for 5 minutes until the apples are soft. Drain if necessary and set aside.

- Divide the oat mixture in half and press one half of the mixture over the base of the prepared tin. Spread the apple and date mixture over the oat layer. Top with the remaining oat mixture, spreading evenly.

- Bake for about 30 minutes until golden brown and firm to the touch. Leave to cool in the tin for 5 minutes then cut into 16 bars. Leave in the tin until cold.

# eating for swimming

Swimming is among the top three most popular fitness activities, with around 1 in 5 people claiming to swim regularly. Whether you work out in the pool as part of a cross-training programme or you swim to compete, you'll benefit from a smart eating plan.

What you eat and drink can make a big difference to your stamina, speed and technique in the pool. See Chapters 1–4 for essential information on eating for exercise. This chapter gives you extra tips on eating for swimming as well as answering nutrition questions frequently asked by swimmers. And, if you are preparing for a sponsored swim or a gala, this chapter provides you with a pre-event eating strategy to help you swim faster and further.

## how many calories?

The number of calories you burn swimming depends on which stroke you're using and how fast you're going. Some unfit swimmers swim in such a slow relaxed fashion that their breathing rate hardly increases and they burn no more calories than if they were sitting! Hard swimming, on the other hand, can burn as many as 600 calories in half an hour. The table below shows you approximately how many calories you burn per hour using various strokes.

| stroke | cals/ kg/hr | 60 kg | 65 kg | 70 kg | 75 kg | 80 kg |
|---|---|---|---|---|---|---|
| side stroke | 7.32 | 439 | 476 | 512 | 549 | 586 |
| slow crawl | 7.68 | 461 | 499 | 538 | 576 | 614 |
| medium crawl | 9.36 | 562 | 608 | 655 | 702 | 749 |
| breast stroke | 9.72 | 584 | 632 | 680 | 729 | 778 |
| back stroke | 10.14 | 608 | 659 | 710 | 760 | 811 |
| fast crawl* | 17.1 | 1026 | 1112 | 1197 | 1283 | 1368 |

*Most swimmers probably could not maintain this speed continously for 1 hour*

You can get an idea of how many calories you should be eating by working out your daily calorie burn (see page 65). If you swim for half an hour a day, you'll probably need between 2500 and 3500 calories daily. An elite swimmer would need between 4000 and 5500 calories per day.

**Why do I feel ravenous after swimming? Should I follow my appetite and eat loads?**

Your increased appetite is simply your body's way of telling you to eat. After a hard workout, you need to replace the fuel you have just used. Your appetite probably seems bigger after swimming than after other activities because you are cooler. Other activities that make you hot for a while after exercise dampen your appetite temporarily. Swimming, on the other hand, may make you warm but you cool down far quicker in water so by the time you're out and dressed, your body temperature is back to normal, even cooler. After swimming, eat a carbohydrate-rich snack but choose wisely and don't get carried away! There's no evidence that swimmers need to eat any more food after a workout than runners, cyclists or gym-goers.

## tips for all swimmers

*keep lean*

If you can pinch more than an inch, you need to lose some body fat because it could quite literally be dragging you down. It's a myth that extra body fat makes you a better swimmer. It may make you more buoyant (i.e. able to float) but it also slows you down and reduces your stroke efficiency. Research shows that swimmers with lower body fat levels (below 15% for men and below 25% for women) swim faster.

*carb up*

Carbohydrate is the best fuel for your active muscles so you need to eat between 5 and 7 g/kg of body weight each day (that's 350–490 g in a 70 kg swimmer). But if you spend more than two hours a day training (whether it's in the pool or doing other activities), you will need more like 6–8 g of carbohydrate per kg of bodyweight per day (that's 420–560 g for a 70 kg swimmer). Include at least one fist-sized portion of carbohydrate-rich foods (e.g. potatoes, bread, cereal, pasta) with each meal.

## shun pool-side snacks

Ironically, most snacks on offer at swimming venues are high in fat and sugar – certainly unsuitable for refuelling your muscles after swimming. Faced with a choice at the cafeteria, shun those fast foods, chips, chocolate bars and crisps in favour of sandwiches (with a light filling), fruit, cereal or fruit bars, meal replacement shakes or bars, and smoothies. If your venue doesn't provide the right food, bring your own.

## bring a bottle

It's hard to imagine that with so much water around, you could still get dehydrated. But you do sweat while swimming – it's just that it goes straight into the surrounding water. So, it's important that you drink plenty of water before, during and after swimming. If you swim for longer than 30 minutes, keep a water bottle on the poolside, and try to have a drink every 20 or so laps. Aim to drink 125 ml every 15 to 20 minutes. Begin drinking early and before you feel thirsty.

## change your drink

If you swim for longer than an hour, swapping your water for a sports drink containing 4–8 g carbohydrate per 100 ml (or juice diluted one to one with water) will make swimming feel easier and help you keep going longer. You'll need to start drinking within the first 30 minutes as it takes around 30 minutes for those carbs to reach your muscles. Try different drinks until you find one that you like. If some sit heavy in your stomach, you may need to reduce the strength by mixing them with extra water.

## hit the snack bar

After a hard swim, you need to replace your energy stores by having a carbohydrate-rich snack. Eating around 1 g of carbohydrate per kg of your bodyweight (that's 70 g if you weigh 70 kg) within 30 minutes after your swim will speed glycogen recovery. Wait longer than two hours and you'll feel tired during swimming the following day. Have a little protein in your snack too as this increases glycogen storage and allows your muscles to repair faster. Aim for a ratio of about 1 g of protein to 3 g of carbohydrate. Try any of the suggestions in the box below.

## after-swimming snacks

*Include at least 2 cups of water with solid food.*

- sandwich, roll or bagel with chicken or thinly sliced cheese
- baked beans on toast
- meal replacement shake
- cereal, breakfast or nutrition sports bar*
- scones or fruit buns
- fresh fruit and yoghurt

\* choose varieties that contain no hydrogenated fat

**I normally swim first thing in the morning before breakfast and before work. Am I burning more fat this way or would I be better off eating something before I get to the pool?**

The answer depends whether you are swimming primarily to lose weight or to increase your fitness. By swimming on an empty stomach you won't necessarily burn more calories but, over time, you could burn more fat. With low insulin levels in your bloodstream, you can theoretically force your body to use more fat for fuel. The downside, though, is that you may run out of energy. If you slow down sooner than you'd like, maybe you could try having a glass of juice, a sports drink, a meal replacement shake or a slice of toast and jam before you start swimming to boost your intensity and endurance. However, if you have plenty of energy for that early morning swim and you're getting results, stick with what you're doing.

## banana and raisin muffins

*These tasty muffins make ideal snacks after a swim workout. They provide carbohydrate, a little healthy fat (monounsaturated), fibre and vitamins.*

**makes 12**

200 g (7 oz) self raising flour
85 g (3 oz) sugar
pinch of salt
grated zest and juice of 1 orange
4 tablespoons (60 ml) rapeseed or
  sunflower oil
1 egg
125 ml (4 fl oz) skimmed milk
2 large ripe bananas, mashed
60 g (2 oz) raisins

- Pre-heat the oven to 200°C/400°F/Gas mark 6. Line 12 muffin tins with paper muffin cases or oil the tins well.

- Place the flour, sugar, salt and orange zest in a large bowl and mix together.

- In a separate bowl, mix together the oil, egg and milk then pour into the flour mixture and stir until just combined.

- Add the bananas and raisins and stir until just blended.

- Spoon the mixture into the prepared muffin tins – about two-thirds full – and then bake for about 20 minutes until the muffins are risen and golden.

# preparing for a sponsored swim or gala

Preparing for a long swimming event, such as a sponsored swim or a gala, in which you'll be racing several heats in one day requires a smart nutrition strategy. You may burn several hundred calories and that will take its toll on your energy reserves. But by ensuring your glycogen stores are fully stocked and your body is properly hydrated, you'll be able to put in your best performance on the day!

# a few weeks before

## *shed the blubber*

If you need to shed some body fat, now is the time to adjust your diet and training. Count on losing between ½ kg (1 lb) and 1 kg (2 lb) of body fat per week and then work out how long you need to reach your target weight. As you need to create a deficit of 3500 calories to lose half a kilo (1 lb), you should step up your training and cut back on your calorie intake. Save calories by cutting back on foods that contain saturated and hydrogenated fat and/or lots of sugar, such as biscuits, chocolate bars, puddings and savoury snacks. Include other cardiovascular activities to burn fat (see page 54) and include some strength training to preserve muscle and increase your metabolism (see page 95).

## *more meals*

You don't necessarily need to eat more food, but by dividing your daily intake into several small meals and snacks (e.g. three meals and two or three snacks) you'll ensure that all of the calories you eat are used for fuel and not for fat storage. You'll also get a more continuous supply of nutrients, better energy levels and less hunger between meals.

## *go for five*

Getting enough fruit and vegetables is even more important once you step up your training intensity. Are you eating five portions or more a day? Fruit and vegetables provide lots of vitamins and minerals (needed to keep your immune system strong during stressful periods) as well as antioxidant phytonutrients that help combat the extra free radicals produced during intense workouts.

## *get a drinking habit*

If you're planning to be in the pool for more than 30 minutes, you need to practise sipping from a water bottle between laps. Work out how much you can drink (a few sips at a time would be fine) and which drinks suits you best. As a rule of thumb, water is fine for events lasting less than an hour, but if you'll be swimming for longer then sports drinks or diluted juice (in a ratio of 1 part juice to 1 part water) may help keep your energy levels up longer.

## sample meal plan for a swimmer

**breakfast:**            2 slices of wholewheat toast spread with
                          1 tbsp honey
                          fruit smoothie (see recipe on pages xx147)
                          or meal replacement shake

**morning snack:**        raisin bread or Banana and Raisin Muffin
                          (see recipe on page 143)
                          grapes or satsumas

**lunch:**                pasta with tomato sauce topped with 2 tbsp
                          grated cheese
                          salad with 1 tbsp olive/walnut/flaxseed oil
                          apple (or other fresh fruit)

**afternoon snack:**      1 nutrition or cereal bar
                          handful of nuts

**evening meal:**         prawn and vegetable stir-fry with sesame oil
                          cooked wholegrain rice or noodles
                          fruit crumble with low fat custard

**daily totals:**
2600 calories; 412 g carbohydrate; 84 g protein; 79 g fat

# the week before

Carbohydrate loading, practised by endurance athletes to increase their muscle glycogen levels above normal, is not relevant for most swimming competitions. Unless you plan to swim for more than one and a half hours continuously, you are not likely to run out of glycogen. However, ensuring that you have normal or 'full' glycogen stores in your muscles will help you swim longer (in the case of a sponsored swim) or swim faster (in the case of a gala).

## get out of the pool

For the last two or three days of the week, cut back on your training and then rest completely for the last day or two. This will allow the carbohydrate you eat to be stored as glycogen and not be burned during a workout.

## stay balanced

Eating a balanced diet is really all you need to do during the last week. Providing you ease back on your training, you'll allow your muscles to fill out with glycogen. Keep your total fat intake low and focus on slow-release (low GI) carbohydrates in your diet (see page 9). Continue to eat 2–3 portions of protein a day.

## keep drinking

Check that you don't become dehydrated during this last week. Use the colour of your urine as a guide – it should be pale yellow or almost clear. Aim to drink at least 2 litres per day, and more if it's hot.

# the day before

Keep exercise to a minimum and keep eating smart. You need to top up those muscle glycogen stores and keep properly hydrated.

## eat little and often

Have small meals every 2–4 hours to keep your blood sugar levels steady and fuel your muscles in preparation for the tomorrow's event. Avoid big meals or over-eating during the evening, as this will almost certainly make you feel uncomfortable and lethargic the next day.

## try liquid meals

If you feel nervous you probably won't have much of an appetite. Try liquid meals such as meal replacement shakes (see page 88), milk-shakes, yoghurt drinks or smoothies. Swimmers some-times find that semi-liquid or 'slushy' foods are easier to digest when they get pre-race nerves. Try rice pudding, custard, jelly, pureed fruit, tinned fruit (because it's mushy!), instant porridge (if it's smooth) or ripe bananas.

## say no to a curry

Curries, spicy foods, baked beans and pulses (unless you are used to eating them) can cause gas and bloating so avoid eating anything that may cause stomach discomfort. Stick to plain and familiar foods!

## drink water

Make sure that you keep yourself hydrated by drinking at least 2 litres of water throughout the day. Aim to have at least one cup or glass (250 ml) each hour. Your urine should be pale or almost clear.

**Practice your competition strategy in training – maybe have a simulated competition – prior to putting it in place. If travelling, contact the hotel or venue beforehand to find out what kind of food will be available. If necessary, take your own.**

CLIVE BREWER, SPORTS SCIENTIST
AND STRENGTH AND
CONDITIONING SPECIALIST

## strawberry and mango smoothie

*Smoothies make highly nutritious snacks, perfect when you can't face solid food or you need to eat on the go. This delicious combination of fruits is bursting with vitamin C and beta-carotene.*

**makes 2 drinks**      about 12 strawberries
1 ripe mango, peeled, stone removed
   and chopped
grated zest and juice of 1 lime
about 10 ice cubes

Put the strawberries, mango, lime zest and juice and ice cubes in the goblet of a smoothie maker, blender or food processor and process until smooth. Add a little water if you want a thinner consistency.

## on the day

Your aims are to keep your blood sugar levels steady, top up liver glycogen stores in the morning and keep yourself properly hydrated.

### don't swim on empty

Even if you feel nervous, make sure you eat breakfast. Try a liquid meal (see the smoothie recipe above), a yoghurt, some fruit or a slice of toast with jam. Leave 2–4 hours between eating and swimming. Skipping breakfast can leave you feeling light-headed during your event. As blood sugar levels dip, you'll not only feel weak but fuzzy headed too, as glucose is your brain's main fuel source.

### check out the fibre

You may be better off selecting a cereal with a lowish fibre content. Bran cereals and other fibre-rich foods may cause gas and bowel problems during the event. However, rehearse your pre-swim meal in training so you know exactly what agrees with you.

### have a snack

If you will be racing later in the day, schedule a mini-meal or lunch 2–4 hours before the start. It should be rich in carbohydrate and contain a little protein. Try sandwiches with a lean protein filling, a baked potato with a little tuna or cheese, a light pasta dish or a meal replacement shake.

### drink 2 hours before you race

Aim to have around 400–600 ml of water, a sports drink or diluted fruit juice about 2 hours before the race. This will allow plenty of time for that fluid to get absorbed into your body and then for any excess to be excreted. Check your urine is pale yellow in colour by the start time.

### nibble between heats

If you will be competing in several heats, you will need to rehydrate and refuel during your rest periods. It's best to eat frequent light snacks between heats to keep your blood sugar levels constant. Try to eat and drink as soon as possible after your heat, allowing a couple of hours between eating and swimming. Take frequent drinks of water or, if you cannot face solid food, have sports drinks or diluted juice so at least you'll get the carbohydrate you need. Aim to drink 500 ml after each heat.

### drink during a swimathon

If you will be in the pool for more than 30 minutes, you'll need to drink every 20 or so laps. Place your water bottle on the poolside, and follow the drinking schedule that you used during training. Aim to drink 125–250 ml every 15–20 minutes. Start drinking early and before you feel thirsty. Remember you can become dehydrated even when surrounded by water.

## pack a lunch box (or a hamper)

If you don't know what food and drink will be available at the venue, take your own. Organise yourself the day before so that you have a supply of suitable foods and drinks for race day. Remember; don't eat anything that you haven't tried during training.

## pre-event meals

- cereal (low fibre) with fruit and milk
- porridge with honey
- meal replacement shake
- milkshake
- banana and yoghurt
- toast with jam or honey
- smoothie

## snacks for between heats

- cereal bars, breakfast bars, fruit bars
- sports bars or meal replacement bars
- meal replacement shakes
- small sandwiches, rolls or bagels
- bananas, grapes, apples, oranges
- dried fruit
- rice cakes and crackers
- mini boxes (variety packs) of cereal

# after the event

Well done for completing the event! Before you begin celebrating, think about rehydrating and refuelling your body – your body will thank you for it the following day!

## reach for the bottle

Have at least 2 cups (250–500 ml) of water as soon as you've got changed, or at least within 30 minutes of finishing your event. If you are dehydrated (check your urine), a sports drink or diluted juice with a pinch of added salt will help to rehydrate you faster.

## plan a snack

Kick-start your recovery by eating a carbohydrate-rich snack within 30 minutes after your event. Glycogen is re-stocked faster than normal for up to 2 hours after exercise so take advantage of this opportunity to refuel. Aim to consume around 1 g of carbo-hydrate per kg of body-weight. If you weigh 70 kg, you will need to eat 70 g of carbo-hydrate. A little protein (1 g of protein for every 3 g of carbo-hydrate) increases glycogen storage and helps muscles repair faster. Get this either in liquid or solid form (see 'recovery snacks' opposite).

## enjoy a meal

After you've attended to your immediate refuelling needs, you need to plan a balanced meal for about 2 hours later. It should be high in carbohydrate and contain a little protein and a little (unsaturated) fat. Try pasta with chicken and vegetables, a slice of pizza with salad, or a jacket potato with tuna and ratatouille. Avoid the temptation to pig out on fast foods, which could make you feel unwell shortly after an event.

**Your preparation for your next event or workout starts the moment the previous one has finished. So you must re-fuel by eating carbohydrates and rehydrate as soon as possible. The worst mistake you can make is to skip an evening meal and not eat until the following morning.**

JOHN BREWER, DIRECTOR OF HUMAN PERFORMANCE AT LILLESHALL NATIONAL SPORTS CENTRE

## recovery snacks

*Accompany the following with 1–2 cups (150–300 ml) of water or diluted fruit juice (1 part juice, 1 or 2 parts water)*

- cereal bar, nutrition bar or breakfast bar*
- meal replacement shake and fruit
- fruit loaf or fruit buns
- sandwich with a light filling, e.g. chicken, ham, thin cheese slices
- yoghurt drink
- smoothie

* choose varieties that contain no hydrogentated fat

# INDEX